"Can A Girl Run For President?"

. . . You Have the Power to Influence Your World Around You

"Can A Girl Run For President?"

. . . You Have the Power to Influence Your World Around You

by
Christine Harvey

INTRINSIC
TUCSON, ARIZONA   LONDON, ENGLAND

INTRINSIC
USA
P.O. BOX 26040, TUCSON, ARIZONA 85726 USA
TEL. 1-877-731-6045   FAX 1-520-325-8743
LONDON
20 STATION ROAD, WEST DRAYTON, MIDDX, ENGLAND UB7-7BY
TEL. 441-895-431-471   FAX 441-895-422-565

10 9 8 7 6 5 4 3 2 1

MANUFACTURED IN THE UNITED STATES OF AMERICA
ISBN: 1-931031-03-7

Publisher's Cataloging-in-Publication
(Provided by Quality Books, Inc.)

Harvey, Christine
    "Can a girl run for president?" : Christine
Harvey. – 1st ed.
        p.cm.
        Includes index
        ISBN: 1-931031-03-7

        1. Leadership in women—United States.
    2. Citizenship—United States. 3. Political
    participation—United States. 4. Influence
    (Psychology) I. Title.

HQ1233.H37 2000   303.3'4'082
                            QBI00-500148

ISBN: 1-931031-03-7

Dedication

To Dale Carnegie

A person whose teachings influenced me more than
learning to read and write. A person whose teachings
live on beyond his lifetime.

And to You the Reader

A person whose influence can live on, far beyond
your own lifetime.
Grasp it and cherish it and use it wisely.
The world waits for you.

About the Author
〰〰〰〰〰〰〰〰

- Author of six books on business and leadership, published in 22 languages
- Author of syndicated articles in the *Los Angeles Times* and 100 other major newspapers and magazines
- First woman and first American to Chair a London Chamber of Commerce
- First American, other than a US President, invited to address the Parliament of Czechoslovakia after Communism fell
- Trainer, companies worldwide and the US military
- Former Director, venture capital company
- Past Chair of an investment partnership
- Enterprise Board launched by Prince Charles
- Founder, *The Most Promising Businesswoman Award*
- Founding Benefactor of the International Center of the National Speakers Association and former Council member
- Past international director of Zonta International; 36,000 members in over 60 countries, with United Nations consultative status
- Charter member, Zonta London 2 with Margaret Thatcher, Honorary Member
- Board, American Girl Scouts of Europe NORAGS
- Founding President, Paris / Brussels Chapter of the Professional Speakers Association of Europe
- Sponsor of Toastmasters Brussels Capital Club
- Dale Carnegie GA
- Television and radio including *The Heart and Soul of Leadership* and *Power Talk* for AFN network in Europe
- Talk Show Host, *One on One with Christine Harvey* *...People Making a Difference in Government, Politics and the Community.* Sundays, 2 PM US Mountain Time, 91.3 FM, KXCI worldwide by Internet
- International Editor, *Professional Speaker Magazine*
- Chair, Advisory Board for International Business Studies, Pima Community College
- Businesswoman and Professional Speaker

Foreword

by
Sue Dyer

Many people have worked and sacrificed over the past twenty years to open the doors that allowed women to enter the workplace. I have been such a pioneer.

I found being a woman working in a man's world challenging and exciting, but it did take time to get to know the rules of the game. For the most part I have always been treated fairly and with respect. I've always taught my daughter that she can do whatever she wants. I believed that we have "come a long way baby".

One evening Christine Harvey called me to discuss a speech she was preparing for the Leaders of the American Girl Scout of Europe. She explained that the speech had been inspired by a ten-year-old girl asking her teacher if a girl can run for President. I was shocked!

"You mean that in the new millennium, girls don't know that they can run for President? How could this be?"

Well, I suppose that if I were ten, I would look at the President and see that he was a man, and then look at all the past Presidents and see that they were all men too. And of course no one had ever told me it could be any different.

"Incredible," I thought. "Wow! What messages are we still giving our girls?" I was dumbfounded with the revelation that we have not come as far as I had believed.

The realization kept pounding away at me. After a couple of days I called Christine and said to her, "You have to turn your speech into a book!"

We must help girls, and women too, understand that they can be anything they want to be including President. They need to know that women can do as good a job as men as political leaders, perhaps even better. And we have to start when they are still girls – teaching them and training them for these possibilities.

Well, Christine went to Europe and gave her speech – and it was one of those turning points you always hear about. The audience was buzzing. They stood and cheered. They wanted to start preparing their girls immediately and they left with tools in hand to do it.

And that is how this book came to be. It is a book that enlightens us all; not only about our misconception that girls think their roles are unlimited, but about the steps we must take as adults to role model leadership in our own lives.

It is also a cry to arms, to raise the values in our countries, one person at a time.

It is my sincere hope that after reading *Can a Girl Run for President?*, you will buy a copy for every teacher, parent, grandparent, Girl Scout leader and every other leader of girls you know. Start a *Can a Girl Run for President?* discussion group in your community. And most importantly, start treating girls as potential leaders now. Today. Don't wait, the direction of our societies is at stake. Start with yourself. Our future truly is in your hands.

Sue Dyer, MBA
President, OrgMetrics
URL: www.orgmetric.com

First woman in the US to head a collective bargaining unit in the construction industry.

Acknowledgements

My supporters have been wonderful throughout the writing of this book, and the speech on which it is based. Teresa Gonzalez, my Marketing Director, with her boundless enthusiasm has talked to hundreds of people and organizations – all wanting to support the goals of the book.

My appreciation goes to all those who reviewed the book and the speech and provided inspiration.

To my ex-pat, European and military friends: Hilde Bartlett, Mona Hedstrom, Walter Blackburn, Janet Smith, Nancy and Mike Sandmann, Gloria and Lloyd Lietz, Avril Barker, Eva Hanses-Doyle, Mitch Marovitz, Jean Morgan-Bryant and Mic Bryant.

To my Girl Scout colleagues affiliated with the Girl Scout Board and Headquarters: Jeane Cella and Sandy Thomas. To my Toastmaster friends: Gail Marsh, David Brooks, Mike Monroy, Mike Adubato, and Ranger Russell.

To my Arizona colleagues: Beth Walkup, Lynn and Derek Clark, Sharon Hekman, Donna Reed, Carol Somers, Valerie Phelps, Sharon Mooney Welker, Gail Grossetta, Jacquie McNulty, Patty Weiss, Patti Noland, Starr Cochran, Paula Maxwell, Gladys Sarlat, Karen Lee Rice, Deborah Chah, Colleen Concannon, Barbara Shelor, Chris Tanz, Lisa Nutt and Elaine Richardson.

The visitors to my home during the process: Janet Lim and her husband Kelly, Barbara Schaper, Sam Horn, and Barbara Poindexter.

To my National Speakers and writer friends and colleagues: Sue Dyer and Bruce Wiggs, Kay and Eric Allenbaugh, Dan Poynter, Lou Heckler, Dick Barnett, Naomi Rhode, Glenna Salsbury, Steve Bacque, Joyce Buckner and Lee Robert.

To my family and friends: Tom Harvey, Laurie, Bill, Cheryl and Billy Erskine, Darrin and Brad Braddy, Tom and Yoli Harvey, Rose and Harvey Searing, George Kade, Estelle Kade, Connie and Jerry Kadansky and Angus Garfield.

My gratitude also goes to Jennifer Treece of Office+ for her great editing and sense of humor that kept us going during the last hours, and to Mayra Natchez for her dedication.

And to George Foster for bringing the cover alive with his talent, caring and undying quest for perfection.

And to you the reader, for taking these ideas and spreading them far afield.

- Christine Harvey

Contents

ഏ-ഏ-ഏ-ഏ-ഏ-ഏ-ഏ-ഏ

Introduction
ఈఈఈఈఈఈఈఈఈ

How And Why This Book Was Written

What is the biggest fear you've had to face? For me it was boarding a C-130 aircraft in Germany bound for Bosnia. It wasn't Bosnia that scared me. It was the aircraft. I'd been warned that it had webbing for seats, that it would be stacked with cargo, and that I'd sit knee to knee with soldiers, and that the aircraft may open and drop cargo in flight.

As I sat in the transit bus, I looked at the C-130. It was huge. I couldn't see any windows in it. The warnings I had loomed large in my mind. The longer we sat, the larger they loomed. My high fright and claustrophobia came to the fore. I envisaged the cargo stacked to the ceiling with me sitting under it, no windows and no airspace.

In a minute the bus would pull forward. I still had time to back out. "Should I tell the cameraman to go without me?" I wondered. The feeling of panic was there in my stomach. Luckily the bus idled for 20 minutes and I had time to talk myself to my senses.

I asked a few questions of the soldiers around me, and I made a strategy. I asked if the aircraft had windows. Yes, I was told. One or two small porthole type on each side toward the front. I asked how the seating was arranged, and how we would file onto the aircraft. From that information, I reasoned that I could sit near the porthole windows. That made me feel better.

Once on the plane, I talked and laughed with the soldiers. Yes, we were knee to knee. Yes, there were porthole windows. No, I didn't have cargo stacked above my head.

The C-130 started up. The engines hummed on and on and we wondered how long it would be before takeoff.

Suddenly a silence fell over the plane. I thought back to my father in WWII and imagined how he must have felt going off to a war zone, not knowing if he'd ever come back. That's how the soldiers must have felt, I thought. Most had never been to Bosnia, and they didn't know if they'd ever come back either. My appreciation for our military forces was stamped on my heart forever.

It was different for me. I'd only be there a day or two for the TV special and then I'd be back again.

Over the next day or two I slept in Army quarters, on Army cots. I ate with the soldiers and stepped over rifles as I walked through the mess halls. I interviewed loyal and dedicate officers, male and female. It was truly an experience of a lifetime.

And yet I think back to that moment of fear, and how I could have held myself back. I think of the panic in the pit of my stomach. I think of how I had to talk myself to my senses.

And so it is with everything in life. We have the choice of letting fear let us back or talking ourselves to our senses.

This book is designed to do just that. To let you talk yourself to your senses.

When my son Tom was a teenager, he often remarked that life is not a dress rehearsal. And yet, what do we do with this precious life of ours?

We spend the majority of it holding ourselves back. We miss the incredible journeys of the C-130s, the camp cots and the Bosnia's.

We get glimpse of our geniuses, but we don't move on it. We see things in society that need fixing, but we don't move on that either. Thus, our potential is never realized. And society never gains from our genius.

What if you were to use your full potential? What genius might you discover? What answers might you bring to the world?

This book is designed to let you realize your potential, and let society gain from your genius.

Each day of the week is designed to give you insight. There are inspiring stories from women in America, women who lived under Communism, and women who rose to high positions with little education.

There are action plans to guide you.

There are processes for discovering your credibility and raising it.

There are resources for you to use to reach levels you never thought possible.

Earl Nightingale once said that we can become experts in any subject by devoting seven minutes a day to it. I would like you to become an expert on yourself and your potential. Seven minutes a day, reviewing each chapter will do this.

Each day of the week will have a different impact:

1. On Sundays you'll review why your input is so desperately needed.
2. On Mondays you'll review your own credibility.
3. On Tuesdays you'll be inspired by women all over the world.
4. On Wednesdays you'll choose from three powerful options to increase your credibility and influence.
5. On Thursdays you'll see places to engage and build your leadership.
6. On Fridays you'll select from 10 skills to propel you forward.
7. On Saturdays you'll motivate yourself to use your skills and credibility to make a difference.

As Sue Dyer said in her Foreword, you may want to start a discussion group or mastermind group based on the chapters of the book.

Meet every week and commit to ways you can apply the principles to your own leadership, to your own community, or to mentoring the people around you.

For inspiration on developing the leadership of girls, you'll find ideas in Appendix 1 and 2.

Your actions will inspire others. Your actions will propel you forward. In Chapter Three – Tuesday, for example, you'll read about a 17-year-old mom with little education who became a State Senator and headed up both the House and Senate Judiciary Committees.

The bottom line is this. Chances are you don't need anything more that what you have today to get where you want to go. And each step that you take will help you to influence your world around you in a positive and profound way.

Contact our website for more ideas and let us know about your successes.

Read on and let the sky be your limit.

All the best,

Christine Harvey
ChristineHarvey@compuserve.com

1

Sunday

ԚԚԚԚԚԚ

The Future is in Your Hands

Chapter One

Sunday

ക-ക-ക-ക-ക-ക

The Future Is In Your Hands

It all started with a little ten year old girl who put her hand up and asked her teacher, "Miss Smith, can a girl run for President of the United Stated?" I was horrified. Do girls still have to ask this question? I told my friends and colleagues. They were stunned too. We women think we've come so far. But have we?

Then, I started to look at the state of affairs in the US. I had just moved back from living in Europe. I discovered that some shocking things had happened.

YES, WE CAN DO BETTER

The Wall Street Journal said we have the highest high school drop out rate of any industrialized nation. I wondered, "Are our kids any less intelligent than those I've seen abroad?"

"No," I thought.

Then I looked at crime. Research showed that we had the highest crime rate per population of any country except one. I wondered, "Why are our citizens putting up with this?" Surely this wasn't necessary either.

Then I noticed people complaining about the leadership. People seemed to be throwing up their hands and saying, "We don't like it, but what can we do about it?" It reminded me of the post communist countries I visited where people see leaders as unaccountable.

PEOPLE WANT VALUES

People in the US seemed to be saying, "We want values back in leadership!" I thought of the Colonel I interviewed in Bosnia, Colonel Julie Manta. I was really impressed with her. She was well respected. She had moved up the ladder quickly and had 350 soldiers reporting to her in 6 countries and 22 locations by the age of 39, when I interviewed her for television. She was attractive and genteel. A perfect female leader, I thought. Not the old stereotype of male power.

I had asked Julie what made her move up the ladder so quickly. What principles did she go by? What could she share with younger soldiers, male or female, who also wanted to make their mark?

STOP TOLERATING

She thought a moment. Then she said that she teaches her people this principle: "Don't lie, cheat or steal, or 'tolerate' those who do."

That's it, I thought! Don't 'tolerate' those who do. We've been tolerating too long.

VOTING WITH THEIR FEET

People have been voting with their feet on education. They are home schooling their kids in droves. 700,000 of them. Why, when we have some of the cleverest people in the world here in this country, should we have to go 'outside the system' to educate our kids? We've been 'tolerating' too long.

Colonel Manta's advice was in my mind that August evening in 1998 when the President of the United States was questioned. We had just finished taping the TV special with Colonel Manta in it. I was in Frankfurt, Germany, because that's where the American Forces Television station is based. A German colleague of mine had come to dinner and afterwards we watched television together as the President was questioned.

I remember the room there in Frankfurt. The TV was at the end of the bed, and so we sat there in order to be closer to it. There we were one American and one German, waiting as if the world's future was at stake.

Finally the broadcast started. The President's casualness in drinking his Coke or Pepsi from the can seemed odd. A European would never do that. Certainly not on television. Our country seemed so casual, almost flippant, considering the Oath was at stake.

I was embarrassed. I felt a pit in the bottom of my stomach when I heard, "It depends what 'is' is." I've voted as both a Democrat and a Republican. It wasn't the party. It was the fact that we'd let things go too far. An oath is no longer an oath. We tolerate hair splitting and pretend it's the truth.

"IT WON'T HURT ANYBODY!"

It reminded me of an incident I heard some years ago when four company directors owned a meat packing plant. They had meat that was turning rotten around the edges. They debated whether to sell it or not. If they didn't, they would lose money. Big money. 'If we sell it,' they reasoned, 'it probably won't hurt anybody anyway.' So, they sold it. Afterwards, the press reported that people died and it was traced back to those four individuals.

This is my question. When young people look around, what values do they see that they can take on?

How will they make decisions if there's never a right or wrong? How will that affect you and me?

THE KIDS CAN WAIT?

Not only crime and education, but things that happen around us every day.

My granddaughter was saving her money for weeks to buy the latest Harry Potter book. She looked at the prices on the Internet, and went to the bookstores.

Some bookstores were taking advanced orders, and promised to hold copies for one week. One bookstore took 112 orders. That's 112 kids waiting for their book. However when launch date came, the crowd that came in for books was enormous. They didn't have enough for everyone. However, they did have that stack of 112 books in the back room waiting to be picked up.

"What should we do?" they asked. They decided to go ahead and sell the ones reserved by those 112 kids. The kids would have to wait for the reorders to come in, no matter how long it would take.

I'm glad my granddaughter was not one of those 112 kids. I'd not want to see the look on her face when she went in the next day to pick up that book she saved so hard for. I'd not want to see the look on her face of loss of faith in humanity.

Why? Because I'd like to know that her word will be her bond when she grows up, but it won't be if the role modeling she gets from adults is the lack of trust.

TAKE A STAND

Somebody has to take a stand, I believe. If you agree with me, I ask you to take a stand too. You don't have to call the White House. But you can call the equivalent of the warehouse manager to say you think he made the wrong choice, when you see these things around you.

Why? Not just because of moral values. Tell him he'll lose his customers' loyalty. That will bring it closer to home for him. Do you think my granddaughter or I or anyone we know would go back to that bookstore, had that happened to her? No, you can bet they wouldn't.

PEOPLE BECOME IMMUNE SLOWLY

So who will speak out for values? Who will call it as it is? People turned their back in Hitler's Germany. The movement grew one step at a time. It didn't happen overnight. People became immune slowly. Before long, wrongs looked like rights.

People turned their back when Communism started creeping in. People who lived many years under that regime have said to me, "Government has nothing to do with me. They'll do what they want to do. I have no control."

I'm not saying we're turning into a Nazi Germany or a Communist state, but I am saying we're going in a direction no one seems to want to go.

SEE IF THIS MAKES SENSE TO YOU

Here's my thought. See if this makes sense to you. If we turn a blind eye to everything that's wrong in our neighborhoods, don't you think it spreads like an epidemic?

If we 'tolerate' the lying, cheating and stealing that goes on immediately around us, then it becomes a standard everywhere. Those folks who promised to save 112 books for 112 kids had full intention to do so. But, when faced with a new situation, they turned. That turn caused their promise to become a lie.

They may not look at it that way. They may look at it as selling more books. But, if an action results in a lie to anyone, it is still a lie. And, they need to be told about it.

So who will speak out for values? I believe it's going to be women.

WHY WOMEN?

Why do I say I believe it's going to be women? I'll tell you why. Because women give birth. The female species fights to keep her young alive.

I believe it is the time when women see society dying. Crime is like a cancer. Low education is like a cancer. Women will not stand by and let it die.

A NATIONAL CONVERSATION

They are speaking out, and they will speak out more and more. As they speak out more, a national conversation will develop. As they speak out more, they will develop a following. Their leadership will rise.

And yes, among them a President, a head of state will emerge. It happened in England, it happened in Finland, it happened in Pakistan, it will happen here.

But the question of a woman in the White House is not the underlying question at hand for you and me at this moment. The question at hand now is what are we 'tolerating' which is killing our country now? What are we 'tolerating' which is making the streets unsafe and the schools bad? What are we 'tolerating' at home and at work that needs to be stopped?

HOW EASY IT CAN BE

In the chapters that follow, we'll show you what other women and men are doing to make things right again. How they are speaking out painlessly, to the right people and making a difference. How easy it can be. How little time it takes. How you can speak out and not have negative repercussions for yourself. How you can speak out and let the other person save face.

Yes, now is the time for all good women to come to the aid of their countries! I hope that woman is you. I hope you will join us and help our daughters do it too. Daughters at work, daughters at home, daughters in the community. It's a new suffragette movement, but this time to save a nation, maybe a world.

As I say in my radio and TV programs, "You have the power within you to influence your world around you." Here's how. Go do it.

Now is the time for all good women to come to the aid of their countries.

2

Monday

❧❧❧❧❧❧❧

The Credibility You Already Have

Chapter Two

Monday

The Credibility You Already Have

Many years ago I read a book that was put out by the London Times.

The book said to think of the millions of people in the world. Visualize them. The vast majority are stuck in the everyday rat race. They want to get out, but they don't know how.

STEPPING OVER THE INVISIBLE LINE

There's a huge cluster of those people in the rat race. Visualize them as dots on a page. Notice however that there is some white space on one side of the page with just a few dots on it. It's as if there's an invisible line on the page and very few have found the secret of how to cross over it.

That white side of the page represents freedom. It represents the realm in which you can develop your full potential. The realm in which anything is possible.

FREEDOM CAN BE YOURS

I loved that idea. I read it again and again. One short life to live perhaps. How could I, the person in the rat race, cross that line to freedom and self-actualization?

The answer they said was to acknowledge your strengths. Acknowledge your uniquenesses. Only then can you cross the invisible line.

UNCOVER YOUR BURIED TREASURES

What are your strengths and uniquenesses? Perhaps you've already acknowledged many. But I know there are more. I work with groups often on this. They're always amazed at the treasures they've not seen which are buried inside themselves.

Therefore I'm going to ask you to do an exercise before you get further into the book. It's essential that you discover those treasures buried in yourself. Then, and only then, can you build your credibility.

EXERCISE: CREDIBILITY SELF DISCOVERY

The purpose of this exercise is two fold.

First, it will help you acknowledge your skills and your uniquenesses. You are like *no other* person on earth. You bring an important message to the world. You bring an important slant on the issues that no one else can see.

Second, you'll be able to use the credibility points you identify, in creating change for yourself and other.

Don't be tempted to skip this part! Don't even delay it. If you do, you'll be shortchanging yourself. The few minutes you invest in this will dramatically impact your future.

Take a pen and write as quickly as you can. Use your book or write on a plain piece of paper.

Types of Organizations

List every type of company you've ever worked for, paid or unpaid. Full-time or part-time. Go back to your earliest job. Perhaps it was a bookstore, the phone company, a clothes shop, homemaker, your own business. List everything. Write one idea under the other in columns. Ready go.

-                ·
-                ·
-                ·
-                ·
-                ·
-                ·
-                ·

Good. Now let's look at functions.

Types of Functions

Now list the types of functions in those jobs. Don't worry if you repeat yourself. Just write as fast as you can. Were you in sales, or finance, a baby sitter, a reporter, an administrator? List it down.

•   •

•   •

•   •

•   •

Areas of Exposure

Now list all the areas of exposure you had to other types of jobs and careers. Was your mother or father a cashier? A bus driver? Or a professor? Write that down. List the professions of your cousin, your aunt, your uncle, your sisters and brothers, your neighbors. List any profession you've heard about over the dinner table and across the fence. Write fast.

•   •

•   •

•   •

•   •

Recognition

Good. Now list any awards or recognition you've had. Go back to early childhood, right through to the current day. Awards or certificates. Think about music, sports, school, college, postgraduate, business, organizations, community, competitions. List it.

- •   •
- •   •
- •   •
- •   •

Participation

Good. Now list everything you participated in. Raising children, sports, hobbies, activities you enjoy, service organizations, gardening, keeping fit, traveling, writing, whatever comes to your mind that you do or have done. Write quickly. Let it flow.

- •   •
- •   •
- •   •
- •   •

Competence

Good. Now list anything you do well. Competencies at work and at home. Can you wallpaper a room, motivate people, motivate yourself, change a tire, run a computer? List everything at home, at work and in the community. Don't let your pen stop. Let it flow.

-        •
-        •
-        •
-        •

Preferences

Good. Now list everything you've ever enjoyed studying, either now or in the past. Include normal school, summer school, evening school, professional courses, seminars, books, tapes, lectures, on-line training. List those subjects.

-        •
-        •
-        •
-        •

Enjoyment

Great. Now what else do you simply like to do? Volunteer at school, walk in the woods, be with your family or friends, gardening, Website design. List it.

- •   •
- •   •
- •   •
- •   •
- •   •

All

Good. Now list anything you do well, which you haven't yet listed. Perhaps it's teaching people, creative skills, artistic skills. Put it down.

- •   •
- •   •
- •   •
- •   •
- •   •

Good work! Are you amazed at your history? Look at the wealth of experiences and competencies you have to draw upon.

Look through your list now. Put a circle around three of the points you've written in any box. Circle your three favorite things that jump off the page at you. Circle things that make your heart sing. You can circle more than three if you like, but do at least three.

ACKNOWLEDGING YOUR SKILLS

OK, now go back and write a skill down next to each circle. A skill you gained from that experience. Perhaps you raised a child and learned how to do 10 things at once. That's an organizational skill. Perhaps you won the most promising young musician award and learned to practice every night. That's discipline. Ready. Do that now. Do it for each of your three circles, or more if you circled more.

ACKNOWLEDGING YOUR QUALITIES

Good. Now go back to your circled points one last time. This time think of the quality you possess which propelled you to do whatever you circled. Write that quality next to the circle. Qualities like courage, conviction, determination, integrity, tenacity, passion. Write a quality now next to each circle. Take your time and don't be modest.

This is very important. Do you have at least three qualities written down? Good. Now reflect on your skills and qualities. These give credibility.

You will use it to move up the career ladder. Throughout the book, I will be giving you examples of how to do this. You can use your credibility to accomplish so much in life and society.

DRAW ON YOUR CREDIBILITY FOR CHANGE

When you see things in society from now on that shouldn't be tolerated, you can use your credibility to get them changed. As Colonel Julie Manta said, "Don't lie, cheat or steal or tolerate those who do."

From now on, when you see things happening in society that bothers you, take a new slant on it. See how it's stealing from society. Or stealing from leadership, or stealing from ethics and integrity. By reflecting upon your credibility an idea will come to you on how to solve it quickly.

I like to quote from Richard Rodgers of Unity Church in Phoenix, Arizona. He said, "We don't like what's going on around us, but until we're part of the solution, we support it."

By acknowledging your own credibility as you have here, you'll start to rely more heavily on your skills and qualities. You'll be part of the solution. You'll teach others to be part of it too.

Remember, by acknowledging your own credibility, your career will develop quickly and your influence will heighten. Each day you'll become a more valuable resource to the world.

3

Tuesday

❧❧❧❧❧❧❧

Your Own Style

Chapter Three

Tuesday

◈◈◈◈◈◈

Your Own Style

◈ 1 ◈

GOING TO THE TOP

It was June of 1997. My good friend Hilde Bartlett and I were on the high-speed train to Paris following a conference. The next day my husband Tom would join us and we would all go to the Paris Air Show. I had a Press Pass, and the other two would go for client meetings.

YOUNG MOMS

Hilde and I had been young moms when we met 20 years earlier in England. We had met at a night school. I remember walking into the roomful of people and spotting her immediately. She oozed enthusiasm as she talked with those around her.

Since then we developed a best friend relationship and supported each other enormously. She started her own company and became Business Woman of the Year. I'd become an author, speaker and trainer, traveled the world and held many leadership positions. These were things neither of us had envisioned 20 years earlier.

SUPPORTING BEST FRIENDS

Later when I moved to Belgium and the US, hardly a week went past when we didn't talk or fax each other to help support each other's goals.

It's a blessing to have a friend like that. A rare treasure in life.

It had been an interesting morning. We'd been talking about conditions for women during our train trip. We talked about verbal abuse and how it diminishes the dignity of people.

I remember taking my eight-year-old grandson miniature golfing. The man on the next hole said to his group, "Give her another chance, she's just a girl."

'Just a girl.' I was shocked.

IT STEALS FROM SELF-ESTEEM

We felt that there was too much tolerance for verbal abuse among both men and women. In families. In business.

She vowed that she would stop it happening around her, and I did too. Rather like Colonel Manta's philosophy, "Don't lie, cheat or steal or tolerate those who do."

When we tolerate demeaning language around us, whether targeted at ourselves or others, it steals from the quality of life. It steals from the self-esteem of others. It steals from the very relationship of the people involved. It leads to a downward spiral.

THAT SORT OF A MORNING

And so that was the sort of morning it was, that gorgeous day in France on the train together. It was a lovely summer day in Paris, and with time to spare before the Air Show, we decided to go up to the Eiffel Tower. Little did we know then, what would transpire, and how it would lead to us being the focus of worldwide press!

There are three levels you can go up to on the Eiffel Tower depending on your height preference. I have a bit of height fright, so I thought I'd buy tickets to the first and second levels, and see how I'd like it, one level at a time.

We waited in a short line for the elevator, and then the guard started directing us to the level two elevator. No, we explained, we wanted level one first. At that point he went into a rage, shouting at us in French, saying that we had a ticket for level two and therefore we must go to level two first.

HIS RAGE GREW

When we tried to explain, his rage grew. He grabbed us by the shoulders and shoved us a distance of about five feet.

The other guards looked on in dismay.

Hilde and I walked over to another elevator, and that guard, now aware of the situation, let us go up to level one with complete charm and grace.

NOTICE THE PROBLEM

As we were going up the elevator I said to Hilde, "My goodness, that's an example of verbal abuse if I ever saw one!" She said, "Yes, but it's also physical abuse." I had been so caught up in his shouting, ranting and raving that it overshadowed the physical abuse in my mind.

Later that played a big part in my understanding of society's downfall. If citizens don't notice what's wrong, they won't take steps to correct it. And so *noticing* is the first step.

We had a lovely time at the Eiffel Tower. After lunch we headed down the elevator again and as we walked out we looked at each other. Should we file a report about the incident or let it go? Our time was valuable but if we let it go, the guard would abuse others the same way. People have patterns. He would do it again and again.

"It's not good for the reputation of France," I said. "Think of all the tourists from around the world who can have their vacation badly affected."

SPEAK OUT TO THE TOP PERSON

So instead of ignoring it, we asked where the Director's office was and went there at the foot of the tower. The Director was in a meeting, so we wrote a letter by hand and both signed it.

USE YOUR CREDIBILITY

We wanted to have the letter be taken seriously, so we signed our titles. After my name I wrote, Past

Chairman London Chamber of Commerce. After her name, Hilde wrote Business Women of the Year.

KEEP COPIES

We asked for a photocopy of our letter, and kept a copy. After two weeks we had no answer, so we sent it again. We had an apologetic reply back saying that the man would go before a tribunal.

Two weeks later, the world press was in a stir. My secretary, Janet, called me from London. I was in Los Angeles doing some TV work. "Christine, Christine," she said. "The press from all over the world has been calling. They want to interview you and photograph you. They want Hilde's number. The Eiffel Tower is closed. People are striking."

The press said that the guard was fired and his colleagues went out in protest. Thus the tower was closed during the strike. But as the press said it was not the man's first offense, and our actions prevented others from abuse.

Yes, it took a few minutes of our time to file the report. But most importantly, we had to notice the problem, speak up and speak up to the right people.

DON'T WASTE TIME COMPLAINING TO THE WRONG PEOPLE

The mistake most people make is doing what I used to do. That is to speak up to the wrong person.

It's not good complaining to our friends, our spouse, our neighbor. They have no power to make the change. They just become frustrated too. Pretty soon we have a group of frustrated individuals complaining to each other about how awful it is.

As Kim Green owner of Veritas Communications, says, "Know what you want and what you're willing to do. *Know what kind of a difference you want to make.* Then make it."

If we want to change society for the better, we have to make our energy and time count. It takes only minutes to pick up the phone or write a letter to the top person. Yet you can spend hours complaining unproductively to the wrong people. And at the end, what do you have?

THREE PART FORMULA FOR CHANGE

1. Notice the Problem

2. Speak Out

3. Speak Out to the right person—the one with the ability to create change

---

Don't waste your time and energy complaining to friends and family. That only puts society in a further downward spiral.

Think of a problem around you in society. What needs to be done about it?

Think about what part you can play in changing it.

What credibility can you draw upon in your own background, as Hilde and I did when we signed the letter?

Who can you team up with to solve a problem? Notice the problem, speak out and speak out to the right person – the one who can affect change.

Future sections of this book will give you examples and techniques to use.

Use Tuesdays to review the important Three Part Formula for Change.

At the end of each segment of this chapter, you'll find an Action Sheet to help you review and select action steps.

The following segments of this chapter take you on a journey of leadership styles and actions. Use them for inspiration and ideas to adapt to your own life.

Remember to notice the problem. Then speak out. And speak out to the right person.

ACTION SHEET: GOING TO THE TOP

Ideas for development:

1. Seek new friends always. Choose those who stand out in a crowd.
2. Support your friends by setting goals together for personal and career growth. Follow up to keep each other on track.
3. Notice the problem and speak out.
4. Speak out to the top person, the one who can correct the situation.
5. Use your credibility when you speak out. Sign your title or past achievement, such as Past Chairman of Your Organization. Refer to Chapter Two for ideas.
6. Keep a copy of your complaint and send it again if you get no response the first time.
7. Don't waste your energy complaining to your friends and colleagues. That will make you sick, them sick and society sick.
8. Others...

Of the above ideas, which one is likely to get the best results? What percentage increase could you expect if you do this? (Of salary increase, or community change, or quality of life, etc.)

How long will it take to develop the idea?
How long will it take to get results?
Who should be involved?
What date should you start?
What's the first step you should take?

❧ 2 ❧

CARVING OUT YOUR OWN FUTURE

When Sue Dyer was 28, she decided she had to work in a man's world. That was the only way she could earn enough to support her children. She put the word out, and a friend led her to a job in the construction industry. On Monday she would start as secretary to the Executive Director of a trade association. She hadn't typed since the 7th grade. Her only jobs had been part time teaching and working in clothing stores.

TO THE TOP IN 2 YEARS

Read on and discover how she moved up to Executive Director within two years and became the first woman in the US to be head of a collective bargaining unit in the construction industry.

MILLION DOLLAR MINDSET

Today she leads million dollar mediations between governments and industry. When a freeway collapsed, the community groups were at odds with the city, state and federal agencies as to how to go forward to rebuild the freeway. They argued for four years. With only a few days left to agree, they were in desperation. If agreement couldn't be reached, the money would revert to the Federal Disaster Fund.

Sue Dyer was called, and with the expertise she had developed over the years, she brought them to agreement and rescued their $700 million! For Sue, supported by her team at OrgMetrics, this is an every day occurrence.

SEE OPPORTUNITY IN ADVERSITY

Most people back away from adversity, but Sue saw it as an advantage. In the beginning of her career in construction, her boss was hard to deal with. That's an understatement. When she arrived on that first Monday morning, Nine people worked there. But each time the boss went on a rampage, or had a fit of anger, another person quit.

The boss always kept a gun in his desk. Within two months, only she and the office manager were left. One day even the office manager had enough, packed up her things and left. When the abusive boss, we'll call him Steve, came thundering out, Sue had to explain. "She's gone too," she said. "No one can work for you Steve." He asked, "Are you going to leave too?" She answered quickly, "No, not as long as you live up to my terms."

RESPOND WITH FAITH IN YOURSELF

Keep in mind that Sue had no idea this would happen. She just responded with faith in herself to the opportunity.

She said, "Here are my terms: I hire, and I fire. You never raise your voice at me or anyone else I bring into the organization. I set the rules. You follow them. You treat me with respect." He agreed.

Even after making this promise there were still episodes. One day he went into a fit over something connected with Sue.

He grabbed his gun and started ferociously down the hall toward her office. Over the top of his ranting and raving, Sue could hear the new office staff screeching, "He's going to kill her!"

When Steve reached her office pointing his gun, she stood up from behind her desk and said dismissively, "Steve, put that thing away!"

He backed down, started lamenting his dilemma and eventually slumped into a chair, continuing his saga.

Isolated incidents aside, he stayed out of the office for the most part, until one day the Board of Directors had enough, and asked him to retire.

In the mean time, Sue had been doing his job for two years, including sitting at the bargaining table of the trade unions – 20 men and Sue negotiating wages, fringe benefits, and working rules.

YES, YOU CAN BE THE ONLY WOMAN!

"In those days, the tradition was very macho," Sue says. "The men would yell and scream at each other, pound the table and threaten." Sue's collective bargaining unit was composed of 200 construction companies negotiating with the Teamsters, Operating Engineers, Laborers, Plumbers and Carpenters.

Can you see all these hard hat types yelling and screaming and showing their fists across the table with Sue there? Quite a sight. It was then that she decided to develop the skills she calls non-adversarial negotiation.

DON'T BE MODEST, TELL IT LIKE IT IS

At the time the Board decided to ask her abusive boss to 'retire', the organization was in financial trouble due to his dealings. Sue took the President of the Board aside and said, "I've been the one running this organization now for several years. If you think I'm going to rescue this organization, so you can hire another man, you're wrong. I think I deserve a chance. Give me the position, and the title, and I'll show you."

HOLD YOUR OWN

The president stood up for her and proposed it to the Board. They protested. Some thought she should be called Executive Secretary. "No, If I'm going to do the job, I should get the title," she told them. "Give me six months. If you're not happy, I'll step down."

They agreed and wanted to keep her salary as it was. Her boss' salary had been double. "Look, if I have the title and the job" she said, "I get the pay!" They were reluctant. "Look," she said, "How much do you pay the top people in your companies? Steve made this much money, and cost you more through mismanagement. I deserve the same." They agreed. Sue did the job and had them in the black in two months.

YOU CAN CHANGE THE CULTURE

They never looked back and Sue had her opportunity to change the culture. Before it had been ruthless competitors in a cutthroat place. Now it became a place to share ideas. They learned to cooperate. It proved to be good for the industry, and good for themselves.

They were able to advance further. She changed the way negotiations were conducted. She changed the culture between management and labor. People started to work with respect and look for common good rather than starting from the entrenched position as adversaries.

A WOMAN WHO COULDN'T TYPE!

Sue proved she had the power within her to influence the world around her. A woman. A woman who decided to tackle a man's world. A woman who couldn't type and had never had a full time job. A woman who had never dealt with abusive people and when confronted with an abusive boss, stood up to him and said stop it. All the others, male and female, ran the other way.

I asked Sue what gave her this courage. "I had faced the worst thing in my life I could imagine just before going into that job. My little daughter was ill and had been near death many times. My son and I spent months on end at her bedside at the hospital. My husband, my childhood sweetheart, couldn't take the pressure. We were divorced. I had already had to face my worst fears. I found strength I never knew I had," she said. And she still has it today.

EVERYONE FACES ADVERSITY

What's her advice? "Everyone faces adversity, "she said. "Use it as a way to tap into your inner strength." She believes these things come to us for a reason. "You have a choice," she said. "You can be bitter and afraid, or you can tackle it head on."

But for Sue, 'tackling it' does not mean we must use the old stereotype of aggressiveness. Do you remember the famous psychological theory that's been purporting for years? It says that animals and humans respond in one of two ways ... 'fight or flight.' But, Sue Dyer's method, the one that saves companies at their final hour, the method that saved the $700 million disaster fund, is neither fight nor flight.

SHE HELD HER GROUND

Remember when Sue's boss, Steve, came at her in a fury with a gun? She didn't use fight. She didn't use flight. She simply held her ground. She said, "Steve, put that thing down." In her training on non-adversarial negotiations, she teaches people nationwide this. *If you want to succeed, come from the position of refusing to be an adversary -- no matter what.*

Sue's book, *Partner Your Project* outlines this for the construction industry. It was so popular that she has written a powerful sequel for people to use in all aspects of business and life. She's also developing training on the subject. I've seen the wonders that Sue's methods achieve in bringing about a better world.

PEOPLE WANT DIGNITY

The importance of her methods is far reaching. Many people, male and female, want a method for dealing with life which has dignity for all. If we run, as 'flight' suggests, there is no dignity for us. Secondly, it doesn't fix the problem.

My friend Hilde and I could have walked away from our incident at the Eiffel Tower, shrugged our shoulders and said 'so what' when the guard was abusive. That's 'flight.' But millions of other people after us would have been subjected to his whims of physical and verbal abuse, had we not spoken out to the right person to have it rectified.

The other alternative of 'fight', provides no dignity either. Think of most fight situations you've witnessed. Is there ever a real winner? Do the relationships live or die?

People are seeking a new method that starts from Sue's non-adversarial baseline. A baseline of dignity for all.

WOMEN WHO ARE MAKING A CRITICAL IMPACT

Thus we see the critical impact that women like Sue Dyer are making on society at a time when it's desperately needed. A time when crime hinders society, a time when schools are in dire straits, a time when people want streets that are safe to walk on.

Now is the time, as never before, for you to think about your impact as a woman. Speak out for change as Sue does. Yes, you too can do it. Notice the problem, speak out, and speak out to the right person. Change can be instantaneous. And, you will have been the spearhead.

Review the action sheet that follows and see which aspects you can apply to your own life.

Remember, you can be the
only woman and hold your own!

ACTION SHEET: CARVING OUT YOUR OWN FUTURE

Ideas for development:

1. Decide on the position you want, then put the word out.
2. When people are leaving all around you, see it as an opportunity to move up.
3. Don't be afraid to be the only woman.
4. Be gutsy in stating your terms when the chips are stacked on your side.
5. Have high values and constantly seek ways to implement them.
6. Don't let your lack of 'experience' stop you, if you have faith you can do it.
7. Don't use either fight or flight, instead hold your ground.
8. Others...

Of the above ideas, which one is likely to get the best results? What percentage increase could you expect if you do this? (Of salary increase, or community change, or quality of life, etc.)

How long will it take to develop the idea?
How long will it take to get results?
Who should be involved?
What date should you start?
What's the first step you should take?

❧ 3 ❧

NOT GIVING UP ON YOUTH

When Beth Walkup started her job at the Children's Museum, there was only one problem. There was no money. As Executive Director, she would be expected to find ways to create exhibits and keep the museum functioning.

SEE THE POSSIBILITIES

An idea came to Beth. She noticed that there was a high population of "at risk" kids. There were teens who had dropped out of school, who were pregnant or on drugs. Any and all of the worst for kids.

CREATE LARGER THAN LIFE PROJECTS

Beth thought to herself, "I bet these kids have talent. I bet they would really, down deep, love to use this talent and discover their hidden potential." She decided to try a daring project. "Why not bring these kids in from the streets and let them design our museum exhibit," she told her colleagues.

So with two professional volunteers she brought in 12 of these at risk kids. All drop outs. All destined to a short and uncertain future. "They had no self esteem," she said. "They didn't even think they would live another year, so they made no plans. All their friends were dying in gang wars."

USE INCENTIVES

Beth put business systems into place. If the kids got to work on time, which was difficult since they were sleeping on the streets, they got breakfast. If they actually worked instead of sleeping all day, they got points that converted to pay, "It didn't take long for these kids to catch on," said Beth. Before long, they were all coming to work on time and working all day.

MUTUAL RESPECT WILL EVOLVE

Under the guidance of Beth's small team, they learned to recognize and appreciate each other's talent. They started to work side by side and actually encourage each other.

GIVE THEM RESPONSIBILITY

During the eight short weeks, they created a life size aquarium exhibit! It had the smells of the sea, the sounds of the sea and the look of the sea. Not bad for a group which had never been to the sea! They learned from the research and films Beth exposed them to.

The result? At the end of the eight week program, out of the 12 at risk totally 'unrescueable' kids, two went back to high school, two got their GED and two went on to college! Six came back as volunteers. One was hired by the museum for his great artistic talent, which had never been appreciated before. All in a seven week program!

NONE OF US HAVE TAPPED OUR POTENTIAL

What's the moral of the story? None of us have tapped our potential. Neither have those kids. None of us can predict what the potential is of another human being.

Let's think about this for a moment. What if we were to treat others and ourselves with the highest dignity and the highest respect?

TREAT PEOPLE 'AS IF'

What if, like Beth, we treated kids 'as if' we expected then to be leaders? What if we treated them 'as if' we expected them to be President?

Imagine what it would be like if everyone were operating at his or her highest potential? What an interesting world this would be. But you ask, how much effort will this take? I'm busy at work, and I'm tired when I get home. I don't have time for anything extra.

You don't have to become Executive Director like Beth did. What about your work place? What young people do you have there? What if you started treating them with the dignity you would reserve for the future Queen of England? How do you think they would speak?

Why not try it and let us know. We'll post the results on our web site.

COMPLIMENTS ARE STRESS REDUCERS

A colleague of mine once said "If you're stressed, go say something nice to someone. That takes your stress away." What if your new actions gave you a new lease on life!

"Show people the best in themselves and they're follow you anywhere!" I often say to audiences.

What if your new actions made you a life time hero for someone? You would have earned loyalty forever.

Sometimes we just need to raise the bar a bit for kids. Sometimes we need to raise it a lot. When we do, they find their talent. They find their self worth. They become leaders of society, not burdens of society.

If you have a young person in your life, why not sit down and go through Chapter Two with them. If you help them see their own credibility, their self-confidence will go up, their grades will go up and their appreciation of you will go up. Why not do it now? The rewards will be great.

Review the action sheet that follows and see which aspect you can apply to your own life.

Remember, you have the power
to see potential in everyone, especially the youth.

ACTION SHEET: NOT GIVING UP ON YOUTH

Ideas for Development:

1. Link the problem with an overlooked resource in the community.
2. Let people see you expect the best from them.
3. Create exciting projects that draw out people's creativity, and
4. Create an environment in which people can see and appreciate each other's talents.
5. Give people incentives.
6. Treat people as if they are already a pillar of the community.
7. Show people the best in themselves.
8. Others...

Of the above ideas, which one is likely to get the best results? What percentage increase could you expect if you do this? (Of salary increase, or community change, or quality of life, etc.)

How long will it take to develop the idea?
How long will it take to get results?
Who should be involved?
What date should you start?
What's the first step you should take?

⊸ 4 ⊷

D<small>IGNITY</small>: A W<small>OMEN'S</small> T<small>OOL FOR</small> I<small>NFLUENCE</small>

From 1994 to 1996, I had the opportunity to work under an extraordinary role model. She exemplified dignity.

'Dignity,' I felt, was a concept little encountered in today's world. Almost a lost art. Her name was Chief Folake Solanke – a woman who reached heights in her country and in the world that few people reach, male or female.

I met her when I was elected Director of Zonta International, a service organization that then had 36,000 members from 62 countries. Chief Folake was President. She was Nigerian. But Chairing Boards was not new to her. She was the first female to chair the Western Nigerian Television Corporation, and the first female State Commissioner.

One of the things I admired about President Folake was that she used the word dignity often. "We must give this candidate the dignity she deserves," she would say.

But most of all, it was the leadership role modeling I enjoyed. Most people, who chair meetings, including myself until then, seemed to have a real 'task' orientation in doing it. Not President Folake.

L<small>ET</small> E<small>ACH</small> P<small>ERSON</small> C<small>ONTRIBUTE</small>

For every important issue that came before the Board for consideration, she would ask each of us to express our opinion.

Slowly and steadily we would each take our turn around the table. Everything was done with dignity and grace. Each person was heard out, no matter how their opinion differed from the group.

EVEN CONTROVERSIAL VOTES

Rarely, during those controversial votes did anyone interrupt the speaker. No, that was our moment to be heard with dignity, and later we would open it to full blast debate.

LET YOUR DAUGHTER KNOW SHE WILL BE LEADER

I savored those moments watching Folake work. I wondered where she had had her role modeling and I learned that it was from her father. He let her know that she would some day be leader.

Folake had chosen to take a law degree. Later when she thought of opening her own private law firm, she sought her husband's opinion.

Would the people accept a woman with her own law practice? She would be the first in Western Nigeria.

She remembers her husband's supportive reply. "You're just as good or better at your profession than any man. Of course people will accept you," he said.

Think about the two supportive men in Folake's life for a moment. The first was her father. The second was her husband. Is there any co-incidence here?

SUPPORTIVE FATHERS LEAD TO
SUPPORTIVE HUSBANDS

Let's look at the situation in reverse. Psychologists say that women, who have abusive fathers, marry men who are abusive. It's the pattern they are used to. All people are drawn to patterns they are used to.

What's the answer? If you're a father and you want your daughter to have a supportive husband, you must do what Folake's father did. You must BE a supportive father. Even if you didn't have a supportive father yourself, you must learn to be one. You, and only you, can turn the tide in the family heritage.

And so I cherished those years, working as a Director under Folake as President. I saw it as a new kind of role modeling in female leadership. As I sat at Board meetings, I often watched it from a detached perspective, rather as a life event.

We had Board members from nine different countries, and even though we all spoke in English, I sometimes felt as if I was the cultural interpreter. After living abroad for so many years, I could tell what the Europeans meant which was missed by the Americans, and visa versa.

GIVE APPRECIATION TO YOUR ROLE MODELS

But most of all it was watching Folake's genius at spreading dignity that made the experience worthwhile. I used to watch how she would handle the cultural dynamics and the personality dynamics. Afterwards I'd reflect on how I could apply it to my leadership, either then or in the future. Often I'd write her a thank you note and slip it under her door at the hotel where we stayed.

PUT YOURSELF IN THE OTHER PERSON'S SHOES

It's lonely at the top and I wanted her to know I appreciated her grace and her caring commitment. It's important to support each other that way. Just put yourself in the other person's shoes, and then you'll know the kind of support you can give them.

The final role modeling for me, and for the 3500 others attending, was the way she lead and controlled the international convention. As I think of it now, I'm even more struck with the importance of role modeling we give each other. It opens up new horizons and new possibilities.

If you've ever been to an international convention of any kind, especially one in which delegates debate bylaws, you know how unruly that can be.

BRING DIGNITY TO THE MASSES

As I sat up on the platform facing the 3500 delegates and guests, I wondered how Folake would handle it differently than the dozens I've seen in many organizations before her.

She didn't disappoint me. As each delegate came to the microphone, she listened with dignity. She responded with words of dignity. Even when the proposal was considered by most to be extreme, she responded, "Thank you. You are most gracious. We value your opinion and the concern that you've put into your proposal. Thank you."

ACKNOWLEDGE EACH INDIVIDUAL

And so by acknowledging each individual for the dedication they brought to the issue, whether it was popular or not, she brought dignity to the convention.

Like Sue Dyer from the previous section, she chose not to see these people as adversaries. She brought tears to the eyes of the delegates as they heard her caring words.

I said earlier how important role modeling is. I had been asked many times by members if I thought I might someday want to run for President of the organization.

CUTTING DOWN ON CONTROVERSY

Each time I was asked that question, my mind would jump to the convention and I would wonder how I would handle it in a way that was comfortable to me. A way that would cut down the controversy and let everyone leave feeling united.

Folake gave me that role model. She also gave it to 3500 others. All of us can go out and emulate the skills we see, in other organizations, companies and communities.

When we emulate these positive skills, other people start to use them too. We create a positive upward spiral. That's why your participation is so important.

BE PREPARED IN ADVANCE

At the end of the convention, a fellow Board member and I got up and read a tribute to President Folake. That brought more tears to the eyes of the delegates.

We weren't sure we would have the opportunity to present the tribute, but we prepared it in advance just in case. *As so often happens in life, if you are prepared your opportunity comes.*

So in the short time lag while votes were being counted, we gained the time we needed to honor this unique leader. The fellow Board member who prepared the tribute with me was Dr. Ingrid Solms from Germany.

She was the same person who watched the US Presidential hearing with me in Frankfurt and presented a tribute to the female President of Germany together.

START A POSITIVE SPIRAL

Ingrid and I didn't worry about whether this tribute was on the agenda or not. We felt in our hearts that it needed to be done, and we did it. When you look around you, you'll see many similar opportunities to acknowledge the great leaders around you. Your actions will start a positive upward spiral.

LOOK FOR OPPORTUNITIES

Take a minute to think about the opportunities of life around you. What organizations can you join which can expose you to incredible role modeling in leadership? I didn't know where the moving walkway of life would take me when I joined Zonta many years before that.

But you can be certain that in any worldwide organization, you will have tremendous opportunity for exposure to role modeling, for leadership and personal growth.

One thing is for certain. You never know where the moving walkway of life will take you if you don't step onto the walkway.

Remember that using dignity as part of your leadership style, brings high leadership returns.

ACTION SHEET: DIGNITY - A WOMAN'S TOOL FOR INFLUENCE

Ideas for development:

1. When chairing meetings, insist that each person contribute their opinions on major issues.
2. Maintain a decorum of dignity so that each person is heard and honored.
3. Treat your children as if they will be leaders... leaders who use dignity.
4. If you are a father and want your daughter to marry a supportive husband, then be a supportive father.
5. Write notes to leaders you admire and say why you appreciate them as role models.
6. If you are chairing a large controversial convention, use verbal gratitude to all who contribute.
7. Follow your heart. Be prepared give a tribute or any other presentation. If you are prepared, your opportunity will come.
8. Others...

Of the above ideas, which one is likely to get the best results? What percentage increase could you expect if you do this? (Of salary increase, or community change, or quality of life, etc.)

How long will it take to develop the idea?
How long will it take to get results?
Who should be involved?
What date should you start?
What's the first step you should take?

◆ 5 ◆

LET HURDLES MAKE YOU STRONG

If you were a 17-year-old mom, what do you think your chances of becoming a State Senator would be?

DON'T LET MOTHERHOOD HOLD YOU BACK

Most of us don't think 10 or 20 years ahead. We just get on with the job at hand. For Patricia Noland, that was finishing school and later as a single parent, providing a roof over the head of her son and daughter.

Patti wasn't from a well to do family. It was up to her to make it happen. So, as a mom at 17, she went to work as a file clerk for the State of Washington. She gradually got promoted to typist, secretary and finally administrative assistant.

KEEP MOVING UP

At 21, she decided to try her hand at business and went to work for a lumber company as an administrative assistant. They tested people there for computer aptitude. Patti was selected and went off to school for four months to become a computer programmer.

Two years later, she was a single parent with no child support. She moved to Arizona and took a demotion, back to clerk/typist with the City of Tucson, while she waited for a programming job to open.

KEEP GOING FOR IT

All the while, she kept working at her schooling and after seven years, got her AA degree. "It's always a balance," Patti says, "between holding more responsible jobs and being a good mom." But she figured out a way to do both. She moved to a smaller town and became Assistant City Clerk. When the City Clerk retired, she moved into that job.

GET INVOLVED, THEN SEE YOURSELF IN THE POSITION

Then in her mid-20s, she remarried and didn't work for three years. "I got involved with the Republican Club," she said. "I went to all their luncheons and listened to the candidates." She started scheduling the speakers and got to know more and more people. After three years, she became President of the group. "I think sitting there, listening to all the speakers, put the thought in my mind that I could run for office," Patti says.

As so often happens in life, we get a thought and then it materializes! We believe we can, and then we can.

DON'T COMPLAIN IF YOU'RE NOT WILLING TO DO THE JOB YOURSELF

So there she was, only in her late 20's, when someone suggested that she run for County Supervisor. A colleague said to her, "You give half your time to the cause anyway, you might as well hold the office."

At first she said no. But then she started to think. "If I don't step up to the plate and try to do the job, then I can never criticize those who do," she said to herself.

GO FOR IT, YOU'LL ALWAYS GAIN SOMETHING

And so she ran, even though the district was four to one, Democrat to Republican. She didn't win the race, but she did win campaign know-how. And, she won respect and recognition. A good experience, but enough to take away any further desire to run for office.

GET BROAD EXPERIENCE

She also decided to go back to work. As Town Clerk and later as City Clerk of another city, she got experience in all areas of city government, including running the elections.

"We had to do everything from picking the polling places to building the voting booths," says Patti. "It all had to be done according to statutes." She had three staff members then.

As City Clerk, she also had to be present at the City Council meetings. "I had to prepare everything before the Council Meeting, and get documents out to the Council Members. Then, after the meetings, I had to prepare minutes of the meeting and make sure that all the ordinances that were passed, got published and recorded," she said.

That was all new to Patti, but it didn't stop her.

Ten years after her first campaign experience, the opportunity came to run for State Representative, and she won. In the fourth year of her term, a terrible thing happened. Her stepson was shot and killer.

It happened during the holiday period – a road rage incident. It was her husband's only son. Patti had helped raise him. To make matters worse, the offender had escaped.

KNOW YOUR RIGHTS

Luckily Patti knew about the law. During her term of office, she had passed legislation that had enacted the Victim's Rights Act. Together, she and her family and friends raised a $50,000 reward to help find the offender. They appeared on America's Most Wanted and the Oprah Show, and finally, after four years, the offender was caught.

Can you imagine the emotional drain of losing a family member and trying to find a killer! It was during the four months after the murder that a Senate seat opened up. Again friends urged her to run.

IF YOU DON'T TRY, YOU'LL NEVER DISCOVER YOUR ABILITY

She weighted the pros and cons. Her energy was low. Her pain was high. But she reasoned, "If I don't do it, I'd always wonder if I would have won and what I would have been able to accomplish."

She ran and won. During her eight years in the Arizona Legislature, she Chaired both the House and Senate Judiciary Committees and served as the Senate Parliamentarian.

JUST DO IT!

Think about your own life as you read this. I asked Patti if she got a Law Degree along the line. After all, 'Judiciary Committee' sounds like it requires a legal degree. "No," she said. "I just get in and do what needs to be done, and learn what needs to be learned."

I asked if she gets nervous treading new ground and what advice she has for others.

"Yes, sometimes I get nervous or anxious, other times I'm so focused I don't even think about it," she said, "but you should just go and do it either way."

ONLY YOU CAN HOLD YOURSELF BACK

"It's important to understand that you are the only one who can hold yourself back," she says. "If I try and don't get it, at least I tried," is her motto.

YOU NEVER KNOW WHAT INFLUENCE YOU CAN HAVE

During those eight years, Patti influenced the world in many ways. Her successful passage of legislation, in addition to the Victim's Rights Act, included Sex Offender Notification, Lobbyist and Election Law Reform, the Omnibus Child Protection Act, other laws involving criminal justice, and last but not least, the Rewrite of the Arizona Criminal Code!

DON'T LET EDUCATION HOLD YOU BACK

All that from the woman who started out as the 17-year-old mom. No Law Degree. No Master's Degree. No Bachelor's Degree. Just the determination that if she doesn't try, she'll never find out what good she can do.

In January of 1999, Patricia Noland was sworn into office as Pima County Clerk of the Superior Court in Arizona, with over 200 people reporting to her.

Imagine the experience she brings to this position from her days as a typist, her days as a programmer, her days as a City Clerk, her days as a State Representative and Senator, her days as Chairman of the House and Senate Judiciary Committees.

Remember, you'll be amazed where the walkway of life takes you. But you must step out onto it.

ACTION SHEET: LET HURDLES MAKE YOU STRONG

Ideas for development:

1. Are you letting motherhood hold you back?
2. Are you constantly looking for new jobs to move into in order to increase your skills?
3. If you're interested in politics or any other field outside your career, are you getting involved?
4. Are you getting broad exposure in your career field so that you can move up the line?
5. Can you develop more of an attitude that 'only you can hold yourself back'?
6. Are you letting lack of education hold you back?
7. Others...

Of the above ideas, which one is likely to get the best results? What percentage increase could you expect if you do this? (Of salary increase, or community change, or quality of life, etc.)

How long will it take to develop the idea?
How long will it take to get results?
Who should be involved?
What date should you start?
What's the first step you should take?

❧ 6 ❧

USING EARLY INFLUENCERS TO DRIVE LEADERSHIP

One day when Eva Doyle's daughter was three, Eva noticed her sitting on the floor with a doll. "Look Mommy, look, "Sonya said, her blue eyes sparkling. "Look Mommy, I'm a nurse!"

YES, YOU CAN BE A DOCTOR!

Eva knelt down to Sonya, took her face in her hands and said," Sonya, if you want to, you could also be a doctor."

Eva remembers Sonya's reaction as if it was yesterday. Sonya's eyes doubled in size as she said, "Really Mommy!"

Today Sonya is a marvelous doctor in Brussels. Is there a co-incidence that she became a doctor instead of a nurse?

WATCH YOUR EXPECTATIONS

Parent's expectations of a child mark their psyche, positively, and negatively. Research was done on people in prison. The results showed that 90% had parents who said, "if you keep that up, you'll end up in jail."

The power of suggestions is so strong and impacts children's futures. The power of suggestion includes words, actions, and thoughts.

WATCH YOUR WORDS

If someone in your family, school or work uses demeaning language with women or girls, you need to stop them. If girls constantly hear phrases like "She's only a girl," or "Women's drivers are awful," it limits their future.

By contrast, here's what Michael Adubato does to encourage young girls. Mike was The Pee Wee Team soccer coach for ages 6 to 8. Only three were girls.

"One little girl got discouraged," said Mike. "It wasn't because she was a bad player, but she just lacked confidence."

PLAY SMARTER

Finally she decided not to play anymore and so Mike took her aside and said, "Look, these boys are not better players than you. They're just bigger and stronger. If you can't match them in playing harder, then play smarter."

She stayed in and her confidence grew. In one game, a big eight-year-old boy twice her size, came running at her, full speed towards her goal with the ball at his feet.

She thought for a minute. He was too big to steal the ball from by running up to him. She couldn't match his strength. She waited. Then at the critical moment when he was up on her, she stuck her foot out, knocked the ball away and then kicked it down the field!

WIN DESPITE THE ODDS

"When I saw the twinkle in her eye and the big smile on her face, I realized I had helped that little girl. I wanted her to know that she could succeed with her own resources despite the odds," says Mike who lives in Belgium and is an Area Governor of European Toastmasters.

DON'T BELIEVE THAT MEN ARE OBSTACLES

Jo'Ann Ruhl says that her mother, Mary Guarino, made a statement to her when she was 16 which influenced her life forever. Her mother said, "Don't believe what women say about men holding them back. They've let men be their obstacle. The only obstacle is your own mind. Decide what you want and do it, believe in yourself."

Jo'Ann is now a traditional Usui Reiki Master, a featured freelance writer and radio host and is involved in a research project with the University of Arizona Human Energy Systems Lab. "None of this would have happened without that critical input at that influential age," says Jo'Ann.

FATHERS – TAKE YOUR GIRLS TO WORK!

What you expose your daughters to, on the work front, can dramatically influence their likes.

Deborah Chah now owns four companies in property development, real estate sales and finance. When she was 16, she had her first part time job driving heavy equipment in construction in Cleveland, Ohio. She got her start in heavy equipment by riding alongside her dad in their family business when she was only three or four years old.

THE MALL

She got her union card at 18. "I saw all my friends working at Dairy Queen and the mall for $3.75 an hour and knew I could make $13 an hour with my union card," said Deborah. It seemed as natural as anything to drive the equipment because of her family background.

She was only the second female in her Local to have a union card. The other was her older sister.

The heavy equipment was so much a part of their lives, that when the two girls were teenagers, they used to lift their four year old brother up to the second story window of their house in the boom of the backhoe.

Thus Deborah worked her way through college driving huge tractor hoes and road graders – it was second nature to her.

ULTIMATE POWER

I asked Deborah what it felt like to drive such heavy equipment. "Ultimate power," was her reply. "It's that, 'um-m,' sort of power. The larger the equipment, the higher the pay and the hierarchy."

It's a field, she feels, in which men are very resistant to having females. But it doesn't stop 5'4" petite Deborah. She saw it as a way to have doors opened in the industry. The next step could have been to become a survey engineer, civil surveyor or specialized equipment operator, all earning $45 an hour or more.

But after getting her degrees, she decided to sell real estate. "Then I became a project manager and got to use my skills in overseeing the construction as well as the selling," she said.

Next, she purchased the marketing arm of the company, then continued to develop the real estate brokerage, and mortgage brokerage. Finally she started purchasing land and developing homes.

ULTIMATE REWARD

In April 2000 Deborah Chah was acknowledged by her industry as the MHI winner of the 'Best Established Sub-Division' in the nation! Her company sells almost 400 homes per year and has 60 employees in four companies.

Now Deborah takes her own kids to work with her!

CAPITOL HILL

Don't underestimate the value of young childhood experience.

Dee Taylor Jolley worked on Capitol Hill for several years. She arranged to take her lunch hour at 3:00 so she could pick up her young son from school. Then she'd take him back to her office where he could nap on the sofa.

Dee sees everything we do with children as teaching and training. When she'd take her young son to receptions, she'd train him in advance on manners and protocol.

DON'T TOUCH THE GRAPES

"We're going to a reception today," she'd say. "You can't take the grapes from the table until I tell you it's time. This is how you have to behave." And so her son grew up comfortable in the surroundings of government, formal and social.

SOME NEGATIVE EVENTS DRIVE US WELL

The past can be used to produce a positive future. It can happen anywhere in the world. Here's a lesson from Europe.

Silvija Dreimane is Secretary General of Parliament in her country of Latvia.

When Silvija was 14, she won a prize in school that allowed her to go to another country. "You can imagine my joy and excitement," she said. "I wanted to run home and tell my mother immediately."

THE KGB CAME ALONG

That was until the KGB came along and told her that she would not be allowed to go on the trip because she had relatives living abroad, including the United States.

Silvija was shocked and confused. Surely there had been some mistake. "My mother had never mentioned anything about relatives abroad. I thought I had none!" she said. She wondered why she was being persecuted unfairly.

The Communists did this to people they didn't trust, who might leave and never come back. But surely it didn't apply to her, she thought.

Silvija went rushing home that night with a heavy heart. What would her mother say? Would it be true or not?

ESCAPING THE REPRESSIVE REGIME

"When I talked to my mother, she admitted it was true," Silvija said. Her relatives had escaped the suppressive regime. They had gone to the four corners of the free world including Dallas, Chicago, San Francisco and beyond.

Silvija's mother had been ill and had stayed behind. She had not revealed these facts to Silvija because she didn't want to put her in jeopardy should the KGB question her.

"For the next seven hours my mother and I poured through stories and pictures that she pulled out from hiding," said Silvija. "I felt my history became whole."

THAT'S WHY I BECAME A LAWYER

Looking back, Silvija says in no uncertain terms, "That's why I became a lawyer."

That's why now in her political capacity, she's driven to do so much for Latvia as Secretary General.

Old memories of domination die hard. She wants freedom to remain now for her people.

She told me about June 14th 1941, when the KGB moved into her country and gave 40,000 people notice to pack up their belongings.

"Within 5 minutes you must leave," they were told. "Take only what can be carried on your backs." And that started the long march to Siberia, on which everyone she knew of died along the way.

... AND A MEMBER OF PARLIAMENT

These early influences make her work for the good of her country in her parliamentary position. She says, "Women have so much to bring to government leadership."

Maybe that's what men see too, who support having more women in leadership.

What early influencers do you have? No matter how negative or positive they are, you can use them to drive your leadership.

Remember that your every word and every deed will influence the life of someone around you.

ACTION SHEET: USING EARLY INFLUENCERS
TO DRIVE LEADERSHIP

Ideas for development:

1. Tell girls they CAN hold the highest positions.
2. Watch your words and even your expectations.
3. Teach winning alternatives to brute force.
4. Fathers, take your girls to work and teach them about your job.
5. Encourage girls to take non-traditional summer job.
6. Expose children to adult protocol and manners.
7. Turn negative experiences into positive influencers.
8. Others...

Of the above ideas, which one is likely to get the best results? What percentage increase could you expect if you do this? (Of salary increase, or community change, or quality of life, etc.)

How long will it take to develop the idea?
How long will it take to get results?
Who should be involved?
What date should you start?
What's the first step you should take?

◈ 7 ◈

STEP UP TO THE PLATE AT SHORT NOTICE

Sometimes in life, we need to step up to the leadership plate at a moment's notice. Everything we practice today will prepare us for that moment.

Nancy Thompson Kiernan from Scottsdale, Arizona went to her grandmother's funeral in a small town in South Dakota. "I was surrounded by my grandmother's friends and loved ones," Nancy said. "But the most important was my father. This would be his final tribute to my grandmother."

Nancy wondered what the preacher would say to make this a special moment.

Then the disaster came. The preacher stood up and started to speak. He fumbled his words. He carried on awkwardly. Worst of all, he couldn't remember her grandmother's name!

LET PAIN PROPEL YOU FORWARD

"I looked at my father's face," said Nancy. "And I saw his pain."

It was that pain that propelled her forward. She fought back her own tears and stood up. She walked over to the preacher and whispered in his ear that she would take over.

Then she gave her 90-year-old grandmother the tribute she deserved. "As I looked at the relief and satisfaction in my father's eyes," she reflected. "it was worth it. It was unusual, but it had to be done and I did it."

DON'T WAIT FOR SOMEONE ELSE

Nancy saw the problem. She relied on herself to solve it. She didn't wait for someone else to do it and lose her courage. She just did it.

IGNORE THE INNER VOICE

She let her conviction in what was right, triumph over the voice inside which wants to stop us. "What will people think? Who am I to step in where I don't have authority?" the voice says.

The point is, when people in authority aren't doing their job properly, it's harmful to many.

VISUALIZE SUCCESS

Put yourself in Nancy's shoes. See yourself stepping up to the plate to do what Nancy did. The more you visualize yourself taking charge, the more you'll be able to step into the leadership gap when it arises.

The motivational guru, Anthony Robbins, rose to success that way. He went from poverty and low self esteem to advisor to governments, by visualizing himself in that role.

Visualization is a powerful concept. In my 'Power Talk' training videos, I tell about two basketball teams, just learning the game. One team practices with the ball on the court. The other team has no ball and just visualizes shooting baskets.

At the end of the prescribed time, both teams test their skills. The team that visualized getting baskets, scored as high as the one that practiced and didn't visualize!

USING THE FUEL OF ANGER

Have you ever felt blocked by government officials? Here's how Hilde Bartlett turned her anger to power and brought an offending bureaucrat in England to his knees.

Hilde and her partner had been working hard to get their company listed as a government supplier in 1991. They'd seen brochures published by Margaret Thatcher's government, encouraging small and medium sized companies like theirs to apply.

Getting listed involved a lot of paperwork. It seemed that every time they turned in one piece of information, the government official wanted ten more. And so it went, month after month.

But Hilde and her partner pressed on, taking valuable time out of their business to pull together the never ending documents. Still, nothing they did seemed to satisfy the bureaucrat.

DECIDE WHEN ENOUGH IS ENOUGH

After nine months of phone calls and visits, Hilde decided that she had had enough. She put on her red power jacket, got into her car and drove up to the bureaucrat's office in London.

"We've given you everything you asked for," she said sternly. "Now here's your latest request. Three months worth of company accounts."

"Good," the bureaucrat said.

"Does that mean you're putting us on the list now?" she demanded.

"No," he said firmly.

"Why not?" she demanded.

"Well," he stammered, "I don't think your company is big enough."

KNOW YOUR RIGHTS

Hilde was outraged.

"Look at these brochures that Margaret Thatcher's government is putting out to encourage companies like ours," she said, raising her voice. "We've given you everything and we are qualified."

"Nothing you say is going to change my mind," said the bureaucrat.

At that point Hilde decided it was time to let her anger be known. The bureaucrat was wrong and she knew it. He knew it too.

LET ANGER PROPEL YOU

She let anger propel her as she perched herself on the corner of his desk. "I'm staying here until you put us on that list. If you want me out of here, you'll have to call the police," she shouted.

The bureaucrat came to his senses.

"Okay, I'll list your company," he said. And at the same time, he listed the three other sister companies that she owned!

Because of that, Hilde and her partner have been able to more than quadruple their business. Think about what Hilde did. She used her anger, and her conviction of her rights, to propel her forward.

DON'T MAKE THIS MISTAKE

The mistake most people make is to walk away angry. The anger consumes them and they never move forward. The offending party, in this case the bureaucrat, stays entrenched. It's like checkmate.

By standing up to the bureaucrat, Hilde created an opening for her services to the government contractors that needed them. Second, she reinforced the intention of Margaret Thatcher's government to expand small businesses, thus helping to fuel the economy.

Think about your encounters with bureaucrats. Use your conviction when you know you're right. Remember that when you pull people into line who are not doing their job correctly, you're helping those who follow you.

INFLUENCING THE VOTE

Use conviction for speaking out in larger meetings too.

Here's how Lisa Nutt handled it. Lisa has an MBA in Global Management and is a college instructor.

She was representing her department in an important meeting. "There were about 20 of us there to revise the curriculum for the college," Lisa said. "The others were mainly male."

"One gentlemen was very vocal. For every agenda item he had a story from his past experience around the world," she said.

MENTION YOUR CREDIBILITY

She let many points go by, but when he downplayed the importance of foreign language studies for international business, she drew the line." She said to the committee, "In my 10 years of experience, speaking another language has been a strategic advantage many times for me in business."

Notice how she prefaced her statement by saying 'In my 10 years of experience!' That gave credibility to her proposal.

HONOR THE POWER YOU HAVE IN SPEAKING OUT

Then Lisa continued: "I reminded the group that people also learn the culture, traditions and gain a perspective of the society when they learn the language," she said. The group voted to include the language competency, and the gentleman was less vocal after that. If she had not spoken out, the vote would have gone the other way.

Remember to honor the power you have in speaking out.

FACING UNCERTAINTIES

Can you imagine the uncertainties you would face if you were asked to live in six different countries early in your career? Every minute of every day, you would be stepping up to the plate of uncertainty.

Gail Grossetta now runs Grossetta International LLC and does cross cultural counseling. "However, there were many times in my early life when I was unsure what to do," said Gail.

And it's no wonder Gail and her husband and daughter faced many uncertainties. Her husband's military career took them to Argentina, England, Thailand, the Philippines, Italy and Germany.

"But here's how I handled it," says Gail. "I always extended my hand in friendship first." That broke the ice.

Protocol is strong in the military. But imagine facing one protocol of six countries in addition to your own! "If in doubt on any kind of protocol," Gail said, "I found that the best solution was to rely on common sense and good manners." Good advice in any situation.

STAND STRONG FOR VALUES

Henry Blount is the Past Chairman of the Continental Congress of European Toastmasters, living in Paris. "I remember a time when I was Captain of my town's junior rugby team," says Henry. "During the game, one member of our team fouled another member. It was violent and purposeful," he says.

Henry had to decide what to do. If he sent him out of the game, they would have to play the rest of the game one player short. "I decided to send him out," he said. His team played on, and because of Henry's action the morale increased, and they beat their opponent.

"Winning is great," says Henry, "but winning fair is better."

FACE OPPOSITION FIRMLY

Think about what Henry had to do here. As leaders, you'll have to face the potential opposition that Henry had. It might be in the office, Board Room, or City Council.

By standing strong for the values you believe in, you'll draw others to your side. Being firm in your conviction counts. If you're wishy washy, you lose credibility and respect.

Now consider your future. Every time you see the opportunity to step into the leadership gap, do it. The stronger you are in supporting your values, the stronger others will be in supporting you.

DON'T UNDERESTIMATE YOUR POWER

Coreen Hennig had an experience that taught her how much influence one individual can have. "Women especially underestimate their power," she said.

Coreen had been performing since she was three, and had won many acting awards throughout her life. After having a family, seven years had passed when she suddenly found herself in the leading female role of *Kiss Me Kate*.

You can imagine the courage it took after a seven year break. Her four night performances would bring in 11,000 people.

During the rehearsal breaks, the director and other actors would light up their cigarettes in the rehearsal area. The lingering smoke made it very difficult for Coreen to sing.

"Surely if they thought it was important not to have smoke here, they would have done something about it already," Coreen thought.

"I finally decided that no one would be happy with a voiceless leading lady," said Coreen. "I got the courage to say something to the director."

YOUR COURAGE WILL BENEFIT OTHERS

"The next night, he told all of the cast and crew that there would be no smoking in the rehearsal building." That decision holds even today.

In addition, the leading man decided to take that opportunity to give up cigarettes! Coreen's actions ended up benefiting people for years to come.

"That action taught me not to be afraid to speak out ever since," says Coreen who is now a producer in *The Christ Commission* film based on the works of Og Mandino.

DON'T BE STONEWALLED

Lou Heckler, a well known humorous speaker and consultant from Florida, remembers when his son was small and had a variety of health problems.

"My wife and I often felt stone walled by the doctors," Lou said. On one occasion, they noticed that their son was feeling tired easily. Lou's wife thought it could perhaps be a hernia and warned Lou to have him examined standing up.

The doctor examined him lying down and said, "No problem."

BE ADAMANT UNTIL THE END

"When I suggested examining him standing up, the doctor looked at me skeptically, but did it anyway," Lou said.

"I'll be darned," the doctor admitted. "He does have a hernia!"

Lou says, "If you believe something to be true, be adamant about it until the end."

SPEAK UP WITH AUTHORITY

Recently a friend came to my rescue when I most needed it. I was attending a conference when hot coffee spilled on me and gave me a bad burn. My colleagues rushed me to the hospital emergency room.

The doctor prescribed a tetanus shot. However, when the doctor's aide came, he wanted to give me a tetanus shot that included diphtheria serum. My body had gone into shock and I was in no mood to argue.

My friend Kathy Brown, a fellow speaker and trained nurse, stopped him. "The diphtheria will give her more pain and suffering," she said. "Don't you have tetanus without diphtheria?" she asked.

DON'T ASSUME THE PROFESSIONAL IS RIGHT

"Yes, we do," he said. "We just have this handy for immunizing kids," he said. "But I can get the tetanus alone if you want."

We waited five minutes and the deed was done. It took 10 days to recover from the burn so I was glad not to have the needless side effects of the diphtheria shot.

Kathy's advice is this: "Its important to speak up productively. Explaining why you want someone to choose differently, can have very positive results," she says.

When we know what's right, we must speak out. We can't assume that the professional knows what's right.' Even if our intuition makes us question the advice we get, we need to ask.

Remember, we must be prepared to step up to the plate at short notice. When we do, we'll get results for ourselves and society!

ACTION SHEET: STEP UP TO THE PLATE
AT SHORT NOTICE

Ideas for development:

1. Don't let personal embarrassment stop you from doing what has to be done.
2. Ignore the inner voice: 'What will they think?'
3. Visualize success before the possible event.
4. Use anger to propel you forward.
5. Mention your credibility when influencing a note or decision.
6. Speak with conviction on values and others will follow your leadership.
7. Don't be stonewalled and stay adamant until the end.
8. Others...

Of the above ideas, which one is likely to get the best results? What percentage increase could you expect if you do this? (Of salary increase, or community change, or quality of life, etc.)

How long will it take to develop the idea?
How long will it take to get results?
Who should be involved?
What date should you start?
What's the first step you should take?

◆ 8 ◆

WHEN RIGHT IS ON YOUR SIDE

How do you handle public authorities? When Janet Lim from Singapore was only 21, she took on the public housing authorities. "At that time, our government was rehousing all the rural residents to high rise flats," Janet said.

"However, to qualify for the new apartment, it was necessary to show written proof of residency and my disabled brother couldn't do it."

Even the hospital tried to help by calling the officials. "But nothing we tried worked," said Janet.

DON'T GIVE UP

Yet she refused to give up. Finally she thought of the ambulance movement chart, which could prove her brother's residency. "After many more trips to the housing board, the officer finally assigned the new apartment to my brother," Janet said.

And her reward was even greater. When the authorities realized the wrong they had done, they gave her brother top priority on the list!

From this incident early in life Janet says she learned to speak out when 'right' is on your side. "If I had not spoken up for my brother, he would have suffered for the past 23 years without the housing he was entitled to," she said. That training held Janet in good stead. She is now a top sales producer in the her industry in Singapore, at Borneo Motors.

IT'S A FREE COUNTRY

Nancy Faville once owned a business called 'Mrs. Olson's Domestic Engineering, Inc.' It provided cleaning and catering services.

"One day I received notice that I should change the name of my company. The officials said the word 'engineering' could mislead people to think it was an engineering company," Nancy said.

Yet her company's name was a household word in her community. She didn't want to change it. After all this is a free country.

Lawyers told her she should comply. "Don't take on the State, Nancy," they warned her. One lawyer told her she'd need to give him a $10,000 retainer to fight her cause.

"I ignored them all because I knew I had right on my side," she said. "People started sending letters to support me and then the news cameras came out." Radio stations joked at the absurdity, and within three weeks the case was dropped.

BENEFITS WILL BE YOURS

A nice side benefit came to Nancy for believing that right was on her side. The publicity allowed her to triple her locations and double her income!

Since then Nancy has sold that business and now owns RFW-Resources for Business.

HANDLING OFFENSIVENESS

How do you handle people who address you demeaningly? Sharon Hekman never gets offended when someone calls her 'dear'. "I just say, 'Oh, you think I'm so young' and make a joke," she says.

Pam Smith, owner of Re-Design Interior Rearrangement, just tackles it head on. "Once someone I knew very little greeted me with 'Hi Sweetie!'" Pam immediately answered back, "Hi Baby." Pam said his jaw dropped and he said quietly, "Hello, Pam," and has never done it again.

If people are not told that their language is offensive, they often think it's acceptable.

GO TO THE OWNER

Pearl Ford-Fyffe left her vehicle for repair at a dealership. When she picked up the car, she found drug store receipts, ashtrays opened and other signs of personal use.

She immediately contacted the dealership owner, who took disciplinary action with his staff. Pearl spoke out to the right person. She didn't complain to her neighbor and family. She went to the person who could take action. And that's how we create change.

...OR THE TELEPHONE BOOK

Kendall SummerHawk was driving home one day and saw the driver of a City vehicle throw his lunch bag out to the street. "I was furious that a City employee would be so neglectful of the environment," Kendall said.

She went home and opened the phone book. "It only took two minutes of my time to report it to the appropriate department," she said. And she was met with support. "Even the City officials thought it was disgusting," she said.

... OR TO THE PRESS

Louise Clymer, a tax accountant, was working at a precinct election one year and noticed that many of the people named on the voter list had died or moved away more than 10 years earlier. "I worried because I knew this left the door open to voter fraud," Louise said, knowing that anyone could come in and claim to be the listed person.

She mentioned the problem in several meetings and was told 'we have our systems!' Still concerned, she wrote a letter to the press. "This resulted in a lot of media attention and the lists being purged," she said.

THE RIGHT CAREER

Right can be on your side with regard to your career too. You have a right to keep searching until you find your niche. Or as in Reesa Woolf's case, create your niche. Although she graduated as Outstanding College Woman, the career counseling she received was lacking. Nurse, teacher or mother were the three options suggested to her. She chose to be a teacher, specializing in speech.

"The first week on the job as a speech pathologist, I knew I had made a serious mistake," says Reesa.

So I spent the next few years using my vacation days to go on informational interviews. I wanted to discover the options in the world of work, and not make another mistake."

After obtaining an MA and Ph.D., she became a Career Counselor – the kind that she wished she'd had while at college! Because she had interviewed so many people in different industries, she could give insight into countless career paths.

Now she's become an Executive Public Speaking Coach. "I specialize in helping people born outside the United States to minimize their accents. So I've used the speech pathology after all!"

JOB SATISFACTION

Reesa now gets tremendous job satisfaction. "A surprising number of CEOs and CFOs are not confident giving speeches," she says. "I often coach them in their offices on Saturdays, for confidentiality reasons," she says.

"I know I've had an influence on the lives of people when they say, 'Before, they needed a gun to get me on the platform. Now they must shoot me to get me off!'" says Reesa. Her search for the right career was worth it.

A MAN'S JOB

Barbara Mintzer had a different career decision. She wanted to move up the ladder in a pharmaceutical company. At the time, a sales position was 'a man's job.' Barbara had to convince the bosses that she could succeed as the first female in sales.

"I was hired," says Barbara, "but the 'all male' sales force resented the time they would have to spend with me because they 'knew' I would fail.

SHE SHOWED THEM DIFFERENTLY

She showed them differently when she became Sales Rep of the Year, *and became the subject of a cover story for an industry magazine!*

Barbara believed in her abilities and followed her dreams. She opened the door for other women to come in and do as well. It also helped corporations double their employee base by including women in sales.

DON'T GIVE IN TO THE 'GOOD GIRL'

Along the way, Barbara learned another lesson. She discovered that she had to confront her inner conflict. "It was very difficult," she said, "to prove what I could do, and not give in to the 'good girl' in me who wanted to be liked."

Barbara said, "I had to do the best job I could and give up being liked for being respected!"

That, she feels, is the major lesson women need to learn. "In business, we need to be respected. If we are liked too, it's icing on the cake!" she says.

CHOOSE PROFESSIONAL GROUPS WISELY

Ruth Smith was the first female bank officer in the State of Florida. Before she was appointed, she was asked to start a woman's service organization.

"I thought hard about the invitation, and decided that my best move would be to decline the honor and watch for the opportunity to join a professional banker's group, then only men," she said.

"It worked and that was probably one of the most important career building decisions I made at the time," says Ruth.

One of her warmest memories was attending a banking school that had 300 men and five women in the class.

"Three years later when we graduated, several men had been dismissed from the class but the five of us women survived," regales Ruth.

"We were thrilled to receive an unexpected standing ovation from our all male classmates when we walked on stage to receive our diplomas!" Ruth now owns RKS Mortgage.

SOMETHING WILL CHANGE

Carol Larson knew that right was on her side even when chronic fatigue and fibromyalgia kept her housebound for three and a half years.

"I just kept feeling deep in my heart that there was something I could do or take or change," said Carol. She was so weak she often couldn't get out of bed. Later when she had strength to get to the living room, she tried to give piano lessons, but was too weak and tired to sit on the bench.

FIVE DAYS AND ONE FRIEND LATER

"Things were awful," Carol said. But one day a friend gave her wheatgrass powder and five days later she was a new person. Later she discovered magnetic therapy with Nikken, and still later more alternative solutions.

"Today I feel invigorated, full of joy, awesome and full of gratitude," she says as she helps people everywhere overcome their problems through her energy work. She's even created her own business called Good Works by turning the negatives of her past into sources of help for others.

Remember to move forward boldly
when right is on your side.

ACTION SHEET: WHEN RIGHT IS ON YOUR SIDE

Ideas for development:

1. Don't give up even with authorities, if right is on your side.
2. When you have a problem, talk to the owner.
3. Open the phone book, make the call or go to the press.
4. Pursue the right career, and persist in male dominated careers.
5. Confront your inner conflicts about women's traditional roles.
6. Choose professional groups wisely.
7. Keep searching for solutions. Never give up.
8. Others...

Of the above ideas, which one is likely to get the best results? What percentage increase could you expect if you do this? (Of salary increase, or community change, or quality of life, etc.)

How long will it take to develop the idea?
How long will it take to get results?
Who should be involved?
What date should you start?
What's the first step you should take?

◦🔊 9 🔊◦

STANDING UP FOR WOMEN

One of the most enthusiastic army officers I know is Colonel Mitch Marovitz.

He recalls a time in the early days of Bosnia, when he was head of AFN, the American Forces Television in Europe.

"The US forces were moving into Bosnia," he says. "I had an energetic young female reporter on my staff who desperately wanted to cover the story."

Unfortunately her command was against it. They insisted she stay back. They thought the situation was unfit for a woman.

ASK FOR SUPPORT

"She asked for my help," he said. "I knew she was a pro and could handle it. I made sure she was traveling in safety with the MPs. I told her to go ahead and cover the story. She went and her coverage was of award winning caliber." Later he said, "This played an important role in morale of troops and their families."

GOOD FOR SOCIETY

Standing up for women is a good move for society. Often their talent and insight brings a different view of things. In this case it built the morale of American troops during war torn times.

NOTICE THE PROBLEM

Diane Katz worked in a company in human resources and noticed that the salaries of some jobs, mostly held by women, were lower than the marketplace. She recommended raises for those people performing at higher than satisfactory level.

GO NATIONWIDE

When she got resistance, she waged a nationwide campaign in the company to make it happen. It worked. They got the wages they deserved.

Diane says, "I felt really good about supporting a group of professionals who never had support before. In fact the whole department felt good."

I think an important point here is how good Diane's whole department felt. She led the way.

She saw the problem, spoke out and spoke out to the right people.

And, the dynamics of doing the right thing made others feel good around her. Now Diane has her own company, Harmony, LLC, that helps companies reach their potential.

THEY HAVE THEIR OWN PROBLEMS

Alain Petillot is a French colleague of mine from Toastmasters in Paris. He says he's had many occasions to boost the confidence of people, particularly women in the corporate environment.

"This is the advice I give," he says. "First, don't place too much importance on what people say which upsets you. They have their own problems that can explain their attitude."

Alain is right. If we divert our attention to these negative issues, it takes us off course.

RISE ABOVE IT

Instead, think of yourself as a value driven leader, motivating others and speaking out for values. Then you'll rise above the negative words of others. As Alain says, people have their own problems which can explain their attitude.

Alain goes on to say, "Secondly I tell them to reflect on the whole situation." He tells them, "You are good. You know you are. I know you are. Don't let some trivial episode affect you in such a way." Next time you're in a different situation, apply Alain's advice.

DON'T GET EMOTIONAL

Recently I had the pleasure of meeting Irena Belohorsha, a Parliamentarian from Slovokia who shares Alain's view. Irena's advice to women is to not interpret male aggressiveness as you would if it came from a woman.

"If you make that mistake, you're more likely to get emotional which would not be good. It's better to just support each other and don't react, " she says.

Irena thinks that women support each other better than men do. She was a well-known doctor before she went into Parliament and did many TV interviews. That was good preparation for politics.

ACCEPT IT AS A COMPLIMENT

What caught her by surprise was how negative some of her male colleagues treated each other, as well as the women, in public life. "It's not that they particularly seek out women to undermine, but they do it to anyone who seems like a competitor, male or female." she says.

That proves my point, I've often stressed to women. 'Accept it as a compliment,' I say. That attitude gives you confidence.

PLATO!

Guillermo Martinez Casan, a member of the European Parliament from Spain, says that we will know when the world has truly evolved because there will no longer be a need for a quota system. He reminded me that Plato said that a city could not afford to dismiss one half of its intellectual property - meaning the knowledge and expertise of its women.

STANDING UP FOR YOURSELF

Perhaps there will be days when you doubt your own confidence. It happens to everyone. Here's the story of Iva Reichlova of IMTI, the marvelous woman who ran our training centers in the Czech Republic.

"Back in March 1990 I had to make a decision to start my cooperation with Christine Harvey or not. One evening I sat down and put on a paper all the negative thoughts and reasons," Iva says. "I cannot cooperate with Christine Harvey because: I speak no English; I have no money; I never did anything like that; what would the neighbors think; I have a four-year-old child; I am a single parent; I do not have a babysitter; etc., etc. The list was long.

BURN THE NEGATIVITY

When I couldn't remember anything else I burned the list on the balcony of my apartment. The bonfire was rather small; nevertheless it meant a lot. On the very next day, I called to arrange a meeting with Christine."

"She wanted to have a woman coordinate training centers in the Czech Republic and Slovokia. She said she was impressed with my entrepreneurial attitude, energy and positive view of life."

"The rest is history. For the next four years our teams trained thousands of managers and business owners," Iva says.

"Many went on to start their own business, some won business awards in the European Community and many today are in top positions in corporations. Think what I would have missed if I had not forced my mind to stay positive and stood up for myself as a woman."

FINDING WOMEN FOR PROMOTION

One company Director I recall in Europe had a superb way of bringing women into upper management. He started a monthly luncheon and asked each of his managers to bring a female manager who showed promise for promotion. He had great protests. "Oh, we don't have any," they all said. "Well, keep looking until you find one," was his retort.

BUZZING WITH ENERGY

The next month they all found a female manager. "The room was buzzing with energy," said the Director. "The new group, half male and half female, gave the discussions a new turn."

Two things evolved. First the senior managers never had a problem after that finding female managers to promote. They dropped the idea that there were none.

MORE DYNAMIC DECISION MAKING

Second they had more dynamic decision making with female input. As Plato said in his wisdom, who would he so foolish as to ignore half their resources!

Remember that standing up for women
brings rewards to all.

ACTION SHEET: STANDING UP FOR WOMEN

Ideas for development:

1. If your colleagues suppress you, go up the line to a supportive person and seek their assistance.
2. Or, get support from a larger group within the organization.
3. Rise above negative remarks; realize that people have their own problems.
4. Reflect on your worth when you face a negative situation.
5. Interpret male aggressiveness as a compliment.
6. Confront your negative mind talk. List it and let it go up in smoke.
7. Create lunch meetings with a mix of managers, male and female employees, for synergy, dynamic decision-making and management recruitment purposes.
8. Others ...

Of the above ideas, which one is likely to get the best results? What percentage increase could you expect if you do this? (Of salary increase, or community change, or quality of life, etc.)

How long will it take to develop the idea?
How long will it take to get results?
Who should be involved?
What date should you start?
What's the first step you should take?

4

Wednesday

Increasing Your Credibility and Leadership

Chapter Four

Wednesday

◈◈◈◈◈◈

Increasing Your Credibility and Leadership

How much do you let your past influence your future? The truth is, that wherever you are in life now, is of no consequence. It has no bearing on your future unless you let it.

YESTERDAY'S FEARS MEAN NOTHING

When I was 14, my mother wanted me to take a speech class in school and I was so frightened that I almost ran away from home. Yet a little more than 30 years later, I was addressing the Parliament of Czechoslovakia on the subject of privatization. That was a subject I knew nothing about, even 10 years prior to the event.

Did Margaret Thatcher know that someday she would be Prime Minister? No, she didn't even get her law degree until after her twins were born.

A friend of mine now runs a multi-million dollar business and yet I remember the days when it she was afraid to write a business letter. She feared her schooling was inadequate. She had no idea what her future held.

The point is that all of your experiences, today and in the future, can lead to an even brighter future that you can imagine. This chapter will dramatically accelerate this process. It gives you three foolproof ways to increase your credibility and influence. Choose one or do them all. *They are all within your reach.*

KICK START YOUR CREDIBILITY AND LEADERSHIP

1. Take on leadership positions.

2. Gain credibility and influence through writing.

3. Raise your profile through speaking or broadcasting.

◄ POINT 1 ►
TAKE LEADERSHIP POSITIONS

I'll share with you the story about how I came to Chair a London Chamber of Commerce. As I tell you, you may want to take notes of things that cross your mind about yourself and your possibilities. The mind forgets quickly, so write it down immediately before it's forgotten.

I had just started my consulting business in London when a man walked into my office from the Chamber of Commerce. He was in charge of recruiting members and he told us that we could gain customers by joining the Chamber. As we were a new company, it sounded like a good idea.

CHOOSE PEOPLE WISELY

I went to the first luncheon meeting and had decided to go alone in order to meet more people. As usual, I surveyed the room to look for the most interesting people to talk to. Yes, this takes courage and confidence but you can do it too.

LET THEM TALK ABOUT THEMSELVES

I learned from taking the Dale Carnegie course that people like talking about themselves best. You can just say, "Hello, I'm so and so. What do you do?" And that's about all it takes to be a great conversationalist.

You let the other person do the talking, and when you find an area of common interest you can say, "Oh, I've been to Singapore too," or whatever, and let them continue. I used to be timid about striking up conversations, but using this method I never worry. I know that people will enjoy talking with me because I'm interested in them.

So that particular day I saw a group of two or three men who looked especially professional. The room was mostly male and I went over and introduced myself. I talked with one gentleman in particular and then we sat at a large round table and continued talking over lunch. He was a banker and was on the Board of the Chamber. He learned about my consulting business and asked me if I'd like to come and visit the next Board Meeting.

I really didn't know what to expect, but I visited and they asked me to join the Board. I did.

LEARN TO SPEAK OUT FOR RECOGNITION

At each meeting I voiced my opinion when I felt strongly about something. I observed this early in life. *It's the people who speak out that get the most leadership recognition...* regardless of how good their ideas are. So if you have ideas, you'd better put them out there. If you need help with this, refer to Chapter Nine, Point Seven.

There were things about the policy that I felt strongly about and so the Chairman asked me to form a subcommittee and study it.

DO WHATEVER MAKES SENSE

I got together three or four people and we met twice. I wrote a report of our findings.

A few months later the Chairman called me. He asked me if I would be willing to run for Chairman to replace him. "Why me?" I asked. "Well, you did such a good job of Chairing the Policy Committee," he said!

And that, in short, is how I came to hold my first influencial Chairmanship.

There is one small twist in the story you should know. And that is that I turned down the offer when the Chairman first called. "Graham, I don't have time. I have a business to run," I said.

A few days later I was talking to Sue Hall, one of my scholarship recipients, and she told me I couldn't turn it down. "Christine, you're always telling us we have to put ourselves out there. There's no way you can turn this down," she said.

DON'T SAY NO TO LEADERSHIP POSITIONS

Sue made me think. She was right. I'm telling you this story because you may not have a Sue in your life. When you get an offer for a leadership position, you must put fear and excuses behind you.

REMIND YOURSELF EVERY WEDNESDAY

Every Wednesday when you read this chapter, guarantee yourself that you won't turn it down. That goes for promotions too. Think of Sue and me and keep the female leadership chain going. The world needs you. And the benefit to you will be enormous.

YOUR PAST TITLE LASTS FOREVER

When I address groups I always ask them to consider the benefits of a leadership title. I ask them to answer this question, "How long will I be able to say that I'm past Chairman of a London Chamber of Commerce?" The answer – forever.

What if I had turned down that opportunity? My life would be totally different. To think I came so close! Don't let it happen to you.

A few years ago, Tom and I went on an investment trip with a group to South America. On the tour, we had many high flyers. Millionaires, a Swiss banker and oil tycoons. We were to meet Heads of State and Government Ministers.

At every Embassy event, the organizer gave a public introduction of our group. At the top of his list each time was the fact that our group included the Past Chairman of a London Chamber of Commerce.

DON'T UNDERESTIMATE YOUR INFLUENCE

Thus you must not underestimate the influence that you'll gain from having a leadership title. That's why you must not turn it down when it comes your way. I'm hammering the point because I see so many people, especially women, shrink away from opportunities.

Windows rarely open twice, and your mission here is to accelerate your progress. Take it when it's offered. Then send us an email and tell us your experience so that we can encourage other women with it.

Not only will you develop as a leader, it will take you to the next step sooner. If other people have faith in you, you must do them the honor of respecting their faith.

PREPARE YOURSELF IN ADVANCE

There are ways that you can prepare yourself for Directorship. The Institute of Directors in London had a certification course I participated in. That's a wonderful way to learn the legalities and to gain a comfort level. Many similar courses are run worldwide.

Ingrid Flory, a colleague of mine in Sweden, runs two companies. One is Flory Consulting which does lobbying for the packaging industry, especially on environmental issues.

Her other company, Regemus Co. specializes in corporate 'Boardmanship.' She lectures on how to run an efficient Board, the advantages of having a Board for small and medium sized companies and how to deal with entrepreneurial, family companies.

Last but not least, she runs specific training courses for women interested in Board work. Ingrid's companies can be reached in Sweden at (46) 8 717-05-05. If you can't find a course locally, perhaps you'd like a trip to Sweden! While laws differ country to country, a Boardmanship foundation will let you project yourself competently.

Remember, don't turn down leadership positions. In fact, prepare yourself in advance.

◆ POINT 2 ◆
GAIN CREDIBILITY THROUGH WRITING

What else can do to you accelerate your influence and leadership? For me, having six books published in 22 languages has brought enormous opportunities. It has opened many doors.

Was I born a writer? No. Did I study journalism? No.

YOU ALREADY HAVE THE QUALIFICATIONS

What I did, was to emulate the books I enjoyed most myself, and those that were best sellers. Could you do that too? Of course you could.

The two books I found most captivating and motivating were Dale Carnegie's *How to Win Friends and Influence People*, and William Nickerson's *How I Turned $1,000 into a Million in Real Estate in My Spare Time*.

When I read Nickerson, I learned an enormous amount from his personal detailed stories of how he did things. It wasn't academic. It wasn't theoretical. And that's why I share my stories with you.

When I read Carnegie, I felt that he had a personal relationship with me, the reader. He wrote in an easy conversational style – more like talking than writing. He asked questions. He gave food for thought. Then he gave his ideas, and ideas from other people. He built up a case that motivated the reader to take action.

I noticed that other people enjoyed his writing too – about 40 million others in over 50 countries. And so I adopted that style. One of my philosophies in life is to not reinvent the wheel. Instead, take the best of what's out there, and adapt it to your style.

MAKE IT YOUR OWN REQUIREMENT

Now think about your own situation. If you were a university professor, you would need to write and be published. It's part of bringing prestige to yourself and your university.

START WITH ARTICLES

Well, think about this. Why not make it a requirement of yourself, in the profession you're in now?

Start with an article as I did. There are magazines galore that would want your articles. What trade magazines do you have in your industry? They don't usually pay, but when they take your article, what happens? You become a published author. You gain acclaim in your field. You can also use it as a springboard for getting books published later.

Here's what I did to get my first article published. You can do it too. I was working in the computer industry at the time and there was a paper called Computer Weekly. I thought it would be interesting to have an article about women in the computer industry. And I thought it would be something I would enjoy doing.

CONTACT THE EDITOR

So I looked in the front of the paper where it lists the editor's name and phone number. I built up my courage and called him. This is what I said. "Hello James, my name is Christine Harvey. I have an idea for writing an article about women in the computer industry. I work in the industry myself. Would you be free next Tuesday for me to come and see you?"

Guess what he said? He said, "By all means. How about 4 PM." That was all there was to it. I was amazed. I thought it would be harder than that. Everyone told me it was impossible to get published as a first-time author.

DON'T LISTEN TO THE WRONG PEOPLE

Later I realized that I had been listening to the wrong people. I'd been listening to people who had never been published – most of them had never tried. They had never picked up the phone as I did. If it were impossible to get published as a first time author, there would be no authors.

Notice that I asked to go see him. I didn't try to sell the idea over the phone. I remember the advice of a businesswoman in Japan who I quoted in my first book, *Your Pursuit of Profit*. She was – and had been advisor to four Prime Ministers. She said, *"Never write to a person if you can talk on the phone instead, and never talk on the phone if you can visit."*

Here's the next enlightening thing that happened. When I got to James' office, he offered to pay me for the article. Can you imagine my delight? I would have written the article without pay, just to get the byline. My goal was to get my name in print as a published author, in order to raise my credibility.

He was absolutely charming and told me how many words he wanted in the article. He offered to send his photographer out to photograph the women I would feature. Then we agreed on the deadline.

Can you imagine your delight too? This could be just one phone call away for you too.

What's the lesson in this? *Stop listening to the advice of people who have not succeeded.* Start listening to the advice of those who *have* succeeded in whatever area of life you want to pursue.

MOVE PAST SELF LIMITING MINDSET

"Oh," you say. "What will people think if I try to write? Who do I think I am to write an article? I can't write." Here's my advice to you. Get over it. Move past this self-limiting mind-set. This is leadership we're talking about. This is your life we're talking about.

In the July 2000 issue of Oprah's magazine, she was quoted as saying, "I was once afraid of people saying, Who does she think she is? Now I have the courage to stand and say, This is who I am."

GO BACK TO YOUR PASSION

Here's what you need to do. Think of your passion. Either something from your profession or outside your profession. Maybe it's education, or something else.

Jot down your thoughts about it. Perhaps gather up a few other articles for ideas. Get quotes from other people who believe what you believe.

Then call the editor as I did. Or write it up first. You did term papers or research papers at school, didn't you? You can do it again. But this time it will be more fun – and more important. You can inspire the world with your idea. You can make the world a better place.

Make your article 500 to 1000 words. Look at the other articles in the magazine to see what length they are. Put a great title on it, and some catchy subtitles.

Then call the editor of the trade magazine and ask if he or she is interested. They will say yes. Then send it. Chances are good to excellent that they'll print it.

YOU HAVE NOTHING TO LOSE

Be sure to put a few words at the bottom about who you are. Go back to Chapter Two and take some of your credibility points and add them to your author description. Look at the magazine to see how other authors do it. Having your name in print will dramatically increase your credibility. Go for it. You have nothing to lose.

Remember that you can raise your credibility through writing. Your ideas can make society a better place.

⊸ POINT 3 ⊱
RAISE YOUR PROFILE THROUGH SPEAKING AND BROADCASTING

'People are more afraid of speaking in public than dying,' it's said. That was true for Sharon Hekman once too, a woman who rose to be Vice Mayor of her city. She's now a leading consultant who brings together government, political and business leaders of Kazakhstan and America.

She recalls her childhood. "I was afraid of everything – driving through puddles in the car, even parking next to berry patches," she said.

When she married and moved to a new town, she took a job as part of a community action team. "I didn't even know how to make friends. When we had meetings, people talked past me as if I was invisible," she said.

But a simple thing happened which changed Sharon's life. She and two colleagues had to give a presentation in front of a hundred people.

"I had planned to leave everything to the other two, and that went fine until question and answer time," she said. Then a question came which was in her area of expertise.

"At that moment, the three of us were standing on the platform together. My colleague put his hand on my back an pushed me forward ...I lived through it," she said. "And to my own amazement, I found it rewarding."

BITE THE BULLET

After that experience, Sharon was no longer afraid to put her opinion forward. She encourages all women to bite the bullet and learn to speak in public.

Sharon moved on to be Deputy Director of the County Juvenile Court, plus Chair and President of a number of service organizations as well as Vice Mayor of the City. Now she chairs the Arizona-Kazakhstan Partnership Foundation.

YOU CAN CONQUER YOUR FEARS

Think about your situation. If you conquer a fear worse than death, doesn't that put you in a position to propel yourself forward? If you don't have a friend to push you forward as Sharon did, then call Toastmasters or Dale Carnegie and sign up today. You'll never regret it and you'll never look back.

Elaine Richardson said that before she ran for State Representative, she was not at all comfortable speaking in public. "I knew I'd have to learn and friends of mine encouraged me to join Toastmasters," she said. "Within one year, my discomfort was completely gone."

CONSIDER BROADCASTING

Why not go and learn now? If you do, you'll be ready for anything!

If raising your profile through broadcasting sounds impossible to you, you've been listening to the wrong people also.

How often do you listen to the radio? What do you hear when you listen? Is it anything motivating? How much do you hear which is negative or repulsive?

Let me tell you about a realization I had recently. I sat in on a broadcasting class and I noticed two things. First, the attendees were mostly male. Second, the majority was extremely liberal or extremely conservative in their viewpoints. Notice I said extremely.

WOMEN ARE NEEDED

Where was the mainstream represented here, I wondered. The answer – they weren't. And where were the women? They weren't there either.

The media has enormous influence. If we aren't all out there, whose fault is it?

Aren't we letting other people lead, by not being out there? You hear people say it's a conspiracy. But is it? Or is it the simple fact that we women, we average citizens who simply want safe streets and good schools, are not making our views heard loudly enough?

What if I told you that your talk show could be one telephone call away? Now I hear you saying, "Christine, you're going too far." But am I?

Here's an example. Our daughter, Laurie Erskine, volunteered to write a weekly article last year for the local paper, about her childrens' school. She interviewed the third grade teacher one week and the science teacher the next.

A PHONE CALL AWAY

Now think of it. Wouldn't the local radio station love to have a program like this? You bet they would, and that program is just a phone call away.

In the US every city has community radio. They sometimes have over 100 on-air volunteers. Many of these stations offer classes on how to do it. You don't need to know anything to attend a class. They teach you about microphones, sound, FCC regulations and so on.

Most volunteers want to play music and so if you come along and want to do community affairs interviews, they will love you. You need only talk to the program director about your idea. You'll probably be on the air within a few weeks. That will give you time to line up your interviews.

INTERVIEWING MADE EASY

People love to be interviewed. You can write out your questions ahead of time, or ask them to write out the questions they'd like to be asked.

Would you be afraid to do that? Why? It's no different than talking on the phone. Make it intimate, like a discussion across the table. In a broadcasting class I had once, the instructor advised us to think of the listeners or viewers as one person sitting in the living room.

It's as easy as that. Don't think about 14 million people. You're only talking to one person at a time.

Think about the benefits you can bring to society. I've had radio programs on both community and commercial radio in various parts of the US and Europe.

HELPING SOCIETY

Once you learn the ropes, you can do it anywhere too. You could interview the police chief or teachers or anyone you feel has a positive message. Wouldn't that be great for society? You will be increasing your leadership and credibility while bringing values to society.

TRY TV TOO

Impossible you say? I'm reminded again and again that I wasted valuable time listening to people who said things were impossible. Yet when I actually did it – which is very different from thinking about it, or worrying about – I found it to be easy.

When you just do it, doors open as if it's happening magically. No contacts are needed. Just do it.

Here's what happened to me with TV. And you can do the same.

LEARN AT CONTINUING EDUCATION

I'd been interviewed on TV about my books. I'd also taken two classes. One was a night school class in New Jersey on educational programming offered through adult education.

The other was in interviewing class I took while living in London, again through continuing education.

At the time, I didn't know if I'd ever use it. I was just interested in it. That gave me the basics. I've always known that TV was the biggest influence in society, thus my interest.

I wanted to turn from being interviewed, to being the interviewer, but I wasn't sure how to do it. I had no friends in the industry.

THINKING, WITHOUT ACTION, GETS YOU NOWHERE

I thought about it for about two years. Thinking, without action, however is frustrating. You get nowhere.

I finally decided a must take some action. The worst thing that could happen I figured, was rejection. And when you weigh up rejection, verses never following your dream, you realize that the consequences of no action are greater.

GO AGAINST THE ODDS OF THE DOOMSAYERS

So while on vacation for three weeks in Los Angeles, I built up my courage and walked into a TV studio off the street. Yes, it was similar to the way I got my first article published, except that I didn't call first. I reasoned that it might work again, although I knew it was against the odds of the doomsayers.

I asked to see the producer and gave the receptionist my card.

Guess what happened next? The producer came out to see me. I said, "I'm visiting LA for three weeks, I've been interviewed on TV and I'd like to help out on the production side." Then I handed him my three-page biography that lists my credibility points. I urge you to keep referring back to Chapter Two because you'll use this data throughout your life.

"OH, WHAT A COINCIDENCE"

This is what happened next. He said, "Oh, what a coincidence. I need a program host right now. Would you be willing to do some on air work for us?" It's interesting how coincidences seem to happen when you put yourself out there. If I'd stayed in my office just thinking about it, it would never have happened.

And so I spent three weeks in LA interviewing, script writing, and doing front of camera work in the studio and in the field. I loved it and I gained experience in every aspect of program production.

At the end of every TV program you see credits roll by. As we were finishing up the editing, the producers said to me, "Christine, when you agreed to work with us, I envisioned that you would host the shows. But, you've done so much more than I originally expected, I'm going to list you as both host and producer."

And so I got the equivalent of my article byline, this time on TV.

YES YOU HAVE THE COURAGE

I know what you could be thinking now. You can be thinking "Oh, that Christine Harvey has guts. I don't have courage like that."

I'll tell you something. When I was younger, I was so intimidated that I couldn't talk on the phone, let alone walk in to see someone. But consider this. Most people are afraid of things until they try them.

I went to work for the phone company, and got over the fear of the phone. I went to work in sales, and got over the fear of people.

Connie Kadansky is a management consultant who has helped hundreds of people move past fear of promoting themselves and their companies.

"The important thing," says Connie, "is to clearly identify your value to your potential clients." This is true in working with any group or organization. If we know our strengths and how they match the needs of the organization, we can focus on those areas. Our credibility goes up.

We all have to sell ourselves and our services," says Connie. More ideas are available on her website: www.exceptionalsales.com.

DO THIS TO REACH YOUR DREAMS

Whatever you fear, you can get over it too. Just put yourself into the situation you fear and you'll get over it. If you don't, you'll never, I repeat never, reach your dreams. And do you know the worst part of that? You'll be cheating society from having all they can have from you in terms of your potential.

STEP OUT OF THE PATH

You never know where the path of life will take you, or what your potential is, until you step out on the path.

After that fateful three weeks, I had the pleasure of working with AFN TV in Europe. I created a one minute, 40-part series called Power Talk which aired to thousands of American troops and their families in Europe. Later I created the concept for a half-hour special on military leadership in which they sent me to Bosnia, Gaeta Italy and Mildenhall England.

In Bosnia, I interviewed the female Colonel, Julie Manta whose motto is about not lying, cheating or stealing or tolerating those who do that. That led me to this book. The experience of flying on a C-130 aircraft, sleeping on Navy bunks and Army cots, eating in mess halls with the soldier and stepping over rifles, was an experience I'll always cherish.

DON'T WASTE YOUR TALENT

Do you see the picture? Step out on the path. Pick up that phone. Walk into that office.

Courage – yes you need it. No, it's not as hard as you think. NOT doing it is to let yourself down. NOT doing it is to waste the wonderful talent you were given, to bring to this world.

KEEP LEARNING NEW THINGS TO KEEP YOUR CONFIDENCE UP

I'll never forget something Akio Morita said. Mr. Morita was the founder of the Sony Corporation. At age 55, he wanted to learn how to fly a helicopter. His staff asked why.

"Mr. Morita," they said, "you have enough money to hire any pilot you want to take you up." That's not the point, he told them. He said he wanted to keep learning new things in order to keep his confidence up.

KILL YOU OR KILL YOUR SPIRIT?

Imagine it. The founder of a major corporation. If he needs to keep trying new things to keep his confidence up, what about you and what about me?

Look at life head on. Yes, you might get rejected. But again, you might not. And if you do, will it kill you? No. Not as much as not trying. That kills your spirit. Which do you prefer?

Donna Reed runs a program called *Living Your Vision,* which is a blueprint for anyone wanting to break through thresholds and barriers. "I know I've made a difference anytime I see their eyes light up," said Donna. In her workshops and retreats, delegates get books, tools, action plans, resources and support. As one delegate said, "It's a life changing experience."

Donna's company, called Tools for Achievers, stresses that there is a spark of genius and great potential within each person.

The world needs you. We need you out there operating at your highest potential. We need you out there being a positive role model for our daughters, our sons and society.

SPEAK OUT FOR VALUES

We need you out there speaking out for values. We need you out there in the new suffragette movement, creating a national dialogue about values.

Yes, society can be better. Yes, we can make education levels respectable again. Yes, we can reduce drugs and crime.

Your actions now, in whatever small or big way, will add to the critical mass. People will see you as a role model. "Oh, Mary had the courage to do or say such and such, I think I'll do it too." That's what will happen when you step forward.

Go for it. You deserve the best.

USE WEDNESDAY TO REMIND YOURSELF

Look at this chapter every Wednesday. Each time you read it, you'll see new possibilities for yourself. At first, it might seem impossible, later a fantasy. But as time goes on, you'll see opportunities in your own life. You'll create imaginative ways to apply the ideas to your life.

You'll see yourself doing it and then it will happen. You'll pick up that phone, you'll walk through that door, you'll go to that meeting. And then your leadership will influence your world around you. Values will rise, education will rise, crime will drop. Do it for yourself. Do it for your country.

Remember, yesterday's fears mean nothing. Don't waste your talent – go for your dreams. Use leadership positions, writing and speaking to reach new heights.

5

Thursday

❧❧❧❧❧❧❧

Picking
Your Platform of Life

Chapter Five

Thursday

✌ ✌ ✌ ✌ ✌ ✌

Picking Your Platform of Life

When I was invited to address the American Girl Scout Leaders in Europe, I started to research the state of affairs in America. I wanted to see where our future female leaders could make the biggest impact.

CRIME AND EDUCATION - APPALLING LEVELS

When I discovered that US students only place 16th and 19th in the science and math and that the crime rate was second highest in the world, I was appalled. I knew immediately why we had to start preparing girls and women for the Presidency.

WE NEED ALL HANDS ON DECK

We need women as well as men in world leadership. In a crisis, which this truly is, we need 100% of our talent to draw from, not 50% or 60% or even 70%. We need you, the women of the world, to come to the aid of your countries. Women of the world unite. It is indeed time for a new suffragette movement.

I sat on a plane across from the darling young lady, named Jackie. She appeared to be about 13. She fussed over her younger brother and made authoritative remarks to him. It was obvious she was in charge. No parents, just them.

I THINK ABOUT IT ALL THE TIME!

I leaned across and said, "Excuse me, when do you think we will have the first female President of the United States?

Without missing a heartbeat, she looked up and said, *"I don't know, but I think about it all the time."*

She thinks about it all the time. That's interesting. 'Hmm, so the suffragette movement spans all generations,' I thought.

She said, "I think more women would think about running for office if there was more about it on TV and radio." Good advice, I thought.

A WOMAN COULD DO THAT

I told her about the man who appeared on Oprah who, through speaking out got $11 Million to fix the schools. "A woman could do that," she said determinedly. Yes she could, I thought.

Then I asked her, what do you think it will take to get a woman elected? When will it happen?

"It'll happen as soon as they put they're mind to it," she said. How right she was, I thought.

EVEN BOYS KNOW

I asked my eight-year-old grandson, Billy, a similar question. Did he know if we've ever had a woman as President? "No we haven't," he said. "And I know why!"

That piqued my interest. "Why?" I asked. "That's because in the old days when they started having Presidents, they thought women weren't as smart as men. But now they know better, and that's why they want one," he said authoritatively.

A GOLD MINE OF FEMALE TALENT

The point is that everyone knows we have a gold mine of talent out there; talent in the form of women with values and visions for the world. It's up to us all to harness that talent and move it forward as value driven leadership.

LINK YOUR PASSION TO THE PROBLEM

What cause will you get behind? If not education or crime, then what? Look at the credibility list you unveiled for yourself from Chapter Two. Think of your passions. Think of your skills and qualities, and link them to the problems around you.

One woman lost her husband in a train shooting and became an activist against this kind of crime. Later she became a Congresswoman, and could directly affect change.

Another woman suffered from an abusive, alcoholic husband. She left him and raised her two children, then was elected as State Representative and made major strides in domestic violence legislation.

WHAT BOTHERS YOU THE MOST?

What problem do you know about firsthand? What bothers you the most? This is the place where you can use your passion and conviction and influence change the most.

Did you read about the high school student from Sacramento California who engaged in 'indecent exposure' on the stage of her graduating class? As she was called forward to be given her diploma, she opened her robe to the audience, exposing her naked body.

ENOUGH IS ENOUGH

When interviewed later, she said she did nothing to mortally injure anyone. Her mother defended her action and said she was proud of her daughter!

Luckily, in this case, parents made their voices heard. 'Enough is enough.'

One said he'd waited 12 years to hear his son's name be read at graduation and it was impossible in the aftermath to hear anything.

MOCKERY OF EDUCATION

Jennifer Martin, one of the Vice Principals in the school said, "People called to say she was wrong. She did offend. They were concerned about family values and making a mockery of education – an institute that should be respected." The parents asked the school to push for arrest. The result was that the student had to appear in court, and was sentenced with community service hours.

TOO GROTESQUE TO PRINT

Jennifer sees other things happening in schools too. Things too grotesque to put in print. Things that will affect all of us in society. She suggests we visit a school. Then we will be in a position to call in as other parents did to support faculty and administrations in bringing values to the classroom.

If the only parents who call are the ones who support immorality, the educators feel their hands are tied. You need not be a parent to call. Education belongs to everyone.

VALUES IN THE CLASSROOM ARE LEGAL!

Her advice to teachers and parents is this. "Don't confuse religion with values. We may not be able to talk about religion in the classroom, but we can and should talk about values," says Jennifer.

Jennifer, who is listed in *Who's Who Among America's Teachers*, counsels her teachers to realize that the appalling things they hear in classroom chit chat, are often things parents often don't know about. Therefore, it becomes their duty to help kids see the impact of indecent behavior on their lives.

Take Jennifer's advice. Visit a school and let your voice be heard.

USE PERSONAL TRAGEDIES FOR CHANGE

Michael Landwehr is the program director at the radio station where I have my program. Before working there, he was a political activist in the area of disability rights.

He devoted 20 years of his life to the cause. His activist role and his work drafting legislation took him to Washington as a lobbyist and political strategist.

Mike says that passion and personal stories sway legislators more than anything does. "At first I made the mistake of talking more about the critical issues," Mike says. "But then I realized that it was the personal stories, the passion, the way it affected you as a person that's important to legislators."

There you have it! What are your personal passions or even personal tragedies that can be used to create change and help others? Whether you run for office or not, there are ways you can affect change.

THROW YOURSELF INTO IT

Timna Sitzes has a passion for getting people involved in her university. "There was a program called 'Faces' but it had no funding and needed more structure," said Timna.

So all summer she worked with the Student Body President, went to 15 freshmen orientations and enticed 400 people to sign up as volunteers.

Because of throwing herself into the job with passion and creating such response, she was appointed Faces Director.

"During the Information Fair in the fall, each elected Senate Official will address the 400," said Timna. Then each volunteer can prioritize their choice – perhaps they'll become a Senate aid or assist a Programs Director. It's a wonderful way to get involved!"

THAT 'SOMEONE' COULD BE YOU

Elaine Richardson is an Arizona State Senator. She knew little politics when she decided to run for State Representative.

"But I knew a lot about the problems in the state," she said. Her background in real estate helped her understand the problems first hand. Her clients and friends told her about their problems.

Finally she decided someone had to do something about it, and so she decided to run for office under the Democratic ticket.

The main passion that drove her to office was the thought of helping women.

She likes to help people get involved, and so she distributes a Call to Action sheet to her constituents.

From Arizona State Senator Elaine Richardson:

TOP 10 WAYS YOUR VOICE CAN BE HEARD

1. Work on a child abuse or domestic violence crisis hotline

2. Increase awareness by inviting abuse experts and/or victims to speak to your organization

3. Help to build or refurbish shelters

4. Volunteer at a child abuse prevention agency or school

5. Volunteer at a domestic violence agency

6. Donate money or services such as accounting, bookkeeping or training

7. Donate needed items such as computers, furniture or toys

8. Help organize a fund-raising project for a child abuse or domestic violence shelter

9. Mentor or tutor a child

10. Work with your Legislature to help enact laws to assist victims of violence and abuse

---

Look at society around you. Create your own version of her list, according to your own passion.

HELPING SOCIETY AS YOU HELP YOURSELF

1. List things in society that, if improved, would benefit yourself and others.
   •
   •

2. Of the above list, which one(s) are you most passionate about? Circle it.
   •
   •

3. What personal experiences can you draw upon?
   •
   •

4. If you get involved in this, how will it enhance your leadership skills?
   •
   •

5. In what ways will it enhance your leadership profile?
   •
   •

6. What other benefits can you gain? Network, influence, satisfaction?
   •
   •

7. What skills and qualities can you bring to it? Refer to your list from Chapter Two.
   •
   •

8. If you use these skills and qualities, what result could you envision for yourself and society?
   •
   •

CHOOSE YOUR ACTION

Now think about how you will implement this. Perhaps you'll talk to your friends about it. Suggest they get this book. Get in a group together or decide to go it alone. Call your legislator and see how you can help. Call a political party, and get involved. Or, as Sue Dyer suggested in the Foreword, form a discussion group based on this book.

VISUALIZE YOURSELF IN THE ROLE

Elaine Richardson was the first woman from her district to ever be elected to her state's Senate.

"I got my insight about government by going to Washington in my high-school years for a special program," she says. By seeing it firsthand, she was able to visualize herself in that political leadership role, long before she got there.

Since being elected to both the House and Senate in Arizona, she's been able to pass many pieces of legislation ranging from underground storage tanks to domestic violence. Think of how important that early exposure to government was.

SEE IT FIRST HAND

There is no substitute for seeing something first hand. If you wanted to interest someone in playing the violin, would you turn on violin music for her?

Or would it be better to take her to a symphony and let her sit in the front row where she could see, feel and touch the emotions of the violinist?

The same is true for government and politics. Imagine the insight you would gain by visiting the state legislature, hearing the debates, seeing how a bill is passed.

KNOWLEDGE AND INSPIRATION

Paula Maxwell, who administers a political party at the county level says, "You can't beat visiting the State's Legislature for knowledge and inspiration."

She recommends going to the web site for your state legislature. Find out what's on the agenda and the days they are in session so that you can visit. You can also call your state legislature for this information.

In Arizona, for example, the telephone number is 800-352-8404 and the Web site is www.azleg.state.az.us. Your state or county may also have a website or telephone number for information.

THESE PEOPLE WORK FOR YOU

Paula says that some people feel a bit intimidated the first time they visit the legislature.

"But, put yourself at ease by remembering that all these people work for us," she says. "People come and go and it's a wonderful place for candidates to learn the issues," she says.

Paula also recommends getting exposure to local government. "Go to city council meetings and Board of Supervisors meetings at the county level," she says.

VOLUNTEER AT PARTY HEADQUARTERS

As Executive Director of the Republican Central Committee for her country, she's helped many candidates get elected at the local, state and national levels.

"Volunteering at the local level really helps you to understand politics too," she advocates. At their party headquarters they encourage people to walk in and volunteer.

"High-school students often volunteer to work on the computer and do data entry," she says.

YOU'LL GET EXPOSURE

Seth Frantzman was one of those who walked in off the street. "I just walked into the Headquarters and asked 'Do you have a college Republican Club?'

They said 'No,' and I asked them if they were interested in starting one," said Seth. And so he did.

"I hosted a Congressional Forum and brought the Congressman together with University representatives to get both sides talking."

And by taking the job, he got exposure to the high ranking people in the State party, and they came to know him.

Later he ran for Student Senate and won.

... AND EXPERIENCE

"I've never been a super motivated speaker," says Seth. "Yet I liked conveying the message so I use my own style of keeping it short and sweet."

No doubt Seth is on the road to success with that philosophy. As Shakespeare said in Richard III, "It's better to be brief than tedious."

Some nights Seth had to address between 300 and 1,000 people in total.

Thus, by being in leadership he continues to sharpen his skills.

NO AGE LIMIT

All political party's welcome volunteers. You can do everything from stuffing envelopes, to calling, to walking with the candidates.

"And there's no lower or upper per age limit," Paula says as she recounts the story of two children under the age of five, walking with their moms and dads on the campaign trail.

Perhaps you're reading this book for career advancement and you have no interest in politics. And yet there's hardly an area of life that government and politics don't touch.

KNOWLEDGE WILL REWARD YOU

Imagine how richly rewarded your repertoire of knowledge will be when you understand firsthand, the workings of government. Why not pick up the phone today and find out how to visit the branch of government which most interests you. Take a friend or a young person, or go alone.

ONLY A PHONE CALL AWAY

If you can't find the number in your phone book, try the City Hall or State Legislature.

Take every Thursday to develop yourself in the areas above. Earl Nightingale once said "You can be a world expert on any subject in three years by giving it seven minutes a day." Why not become an expert in something that will help society?

Remember, when you use your leadership skills in society, you help yourself at the same time.

6

Friday

Personal Skills You Will Need

Chapter Six

Friday

✍✍✍✍✍✍

Personal Skills You Will Need

Did you hear the story of the young wife who cut the ends off the ham before she cooked it? Her newlywed husband wondered why. "I don't know," she replied when he asked her. "My mother always does it, ask her."

So the newlywed husband asked his mother-in-law. Her answer was the same. "I don't know, my mother did it, and so do I."

Finally the young husband, curiosity peaked, asked his wife's grandmother. "Oh," she replied, "when my children were growing up I had a very small oven. I had to cut the ends off to fit it in the small pan."

LOOK FAR AND WIDE FOR THE BEST ROLE MODELS

And so that's how life goes on unless we change it. All the personal skills you'll need are not likely to have been role modeled by those around you. You'll have to look at how other people around you do things to create success. Then choose from the best.

This chapter gives 10 important, personal skills you will need for success, whether it is in government leadership, corporate leadership or family leadership.

◆ POINT 1 ◆
HELPING PEOPLE BE ALL THEY CAN BE

Zig Zigler, the world-renowned sales trainer and motivationalist, says that he got to where he is today, by helping other people build their dreams.

You might ask, 'How do I do that?' Here's my philosophy. Recently I was asked go give a motivational speech at a moment's notice. I told the audience that this philosophy was responsible for everything I had achieved in life. Without it, I would not have been elected to Chair a London Chamber of Commerce, nor have written six books, nor still be married and to the same person.

SHOW PEOPLE THE BEST IN THEMSELVES

Here's the philosophy. *"Show people the best in themselves, and they will follow you anywhere."*

I gave a speech in Australia once, and a woman came up to speak to me afterwards. In the course of the conversation, I said, "I love that red jacket on you."

Eighteen months later I was back in Australia, walking down the street when I had a tap on the shoulder. I looked around and there was the same woman.

She said, "Mrs. Harvey, you probably don't remember me, but I was at your speech awhile back." Then she went on to tell me that she was going through a very depressed period of her life at that time.

"But every time I felt depressed, I opened my closet and took out my jacket. I said to myself, 'Christine Harvey says I look good in this red jacket.' And that pulled me through."

LESS THAN A MINUTE

Think about how long it took me to compliment her on her red jacket. Certainly less than one minute. One minute in the life of passing ships in the night. One minute with a woman half way around the world - and yet, look at the difference it made.

VIEW YOURSELF AS A MOTIVATOR

But here's the secret. It's not time, it's attitude. I view myself as a motivator. If you start to view yourself as a motivator, your influence and satisfaction will increase enormously. Instead of engaging in small talk, I ask people 'what's your latest project' or 'what's new in your life?' That takes 10 seconds.

GIVE HONEST ENCOURAGEMENT

Then I give them my honest encouragement. 'Wow, that sounds great. Have you thought of doing this or that?'

Let your mind search for ways to enhance it. Two minutes is all it takes to do that.

I've been elected to Boards of organizations by people I've met only once. Years later they come and say to me, "Christine, do you remember when we talked at the convention six years ago? You gave me encouragement and ideas."

YOU MAKE IT A BETTER WORLD

Hope and confidence. If you give people that – and why shouldn't you – they will follow you anywhere. You'll have their loyalty, you'll have their support, you'll have their vote. But most of all, you'll have made it a better world by supporting others first.

◈ POINT 2 ◈
THE POWER OF YOUR NETWORK

If you want to improve education, reduce crime or make any changes in society, having a network will greatly increase your chances of success.

The larger your network, the larger your potential influence.

There may be times when you want to extend your circle of acquaintances quickly.

Here's what to do to build a large network.

1. Go to several events, especially if you're new in town or new to an industry, association or political party. You'll find these events listed in the newspaper under the events section.

GO ALONE

2. Go alone. You'll meet people faster that way.

3. Arrive early and stay late.

4. Take plenty of business cards – put them in your right pocket.

5. Go up to interesting looking people. Extend your hand and say, "Hello, I'm ... "

6. Ask them a question. Something personal, but related to the organization, i.e. "How long have you been a member?" Then, a new sentence, OR "What do you like about belonging to this group?"

7. Find out something about them that fascinates you.

EXCHANGE CARDS

8. Say how much you've enjoyed talking to them.

9. Give them a business card. They'll offer theirs. Put it in your left pocket. Pulling things out of your briefcase or handbag slows you down and looks awkward.

10. Move onto the next person who looks interesting, and repeat it.

MAKE A NOTE TO CALL LATER

11. If you meet people you want to link up with later, mark that on their card. Say to them, "I'll make a note to call you later."

12. Come back and file your cards in envelopes marked with the name and date of the event on the front. Keep the ones you want to contact near the front or enter them into your contact management system.

ARRANGE TO MEET LATER

Here are some important points. Don't spend more than two or three minutes with each person if you want to build a large network. Instead, call the ones you like and arrange to meet with them. You can even organize a large event and invite them all.

When I was new to Tucson, Arizona, I went to several business and political events as well as association meetings. I met a wonderfully wide range of interesting people.

At one of these meetings I had the pleasure of meeting Beth Walkup who was then the Executive Director of the Children's Museum where I live. I interviewed her and a number of others on my radio program. I enjoyed getting to know each of them very much. It gave me an immediate feeling of connectedness to my new area.

I especially liked Beth's enthusiasm and dedication to everything she did which included supporting her husband in his race for Mayor of the city.

HONOR PEOPLE

I wanted to honor her for supporting him whether he won or not. I scheduled a luncheon and invited 20 of those interesting women I had met at the business and political events. In the meantime, he won the election.

The synergy of the group was wonderful. They represented all political parties and areas of business. We decided at that luncheon that we wanted to continue to support Beth in her First Lady position and since then have met on a monthly basis.

MAKE SUPPORT GROUPS DIVERSE

When Beth attended a Mayor's Convention with her husband recently, she discovered that few, if any first ladies had this kind of support group.

The Mayor held a reception for us recently and Beth said, "I was honored to be able to talk about my support group at the Convention. What's so unique is the diversity of the group." Beth stresses to how important diversity is and suggests we all 'stretch our comfort zone' in bringing all people together.

Much more can be accomplished that way because of the increased input and outreach.

You can imagine the great satisfaction I get every time our group meets, knowing that I brought the group together. Think of what I would have missed without networking.

REACH ANYONE THROUGH 3 CALLS

Why else would you want a large network? I once heard that you could reach anyone in the world you wanted to meet through three phone calls. What if you had a rare medical condition? Wouldn't it be useful to have a large network of people and expertise to draw upon?

YOU'LL HAVE CONNECTEDNESS

Or maybe you'd like new friends. One theory of psychology is that our mental well being is related to our feeling connectedness. In Point 6 of this chapter, I talk about resentment. Resentment causes cancer. It separates people. Connectedness brings people together. It heals. Having a strong supportive network creates connectedness.

YOU CAN DO IT

MJ Jensen is Chief Idea Officer of Idea Magic, Inc. MJ's biggest challenge was physical disability from sciatica.

"I was practically bedridden when I moved five years ago, and I knew no one," she said. "I didn't know if I would survive and had to face my worst fears."

NETWORKING MADE ALL THE DIFFERENCE

As soon as she was able to get up, she started working, and joined Resources for Women. "I've had great support there," said MJ. "It made all the difference in the world." Five years later in 1999, she was awarded their Networker of the Year Award, and has friends and clients galore.

Her advice to women is this. "You can do it no matter what, even though you don't believe it now."

Your leadership depends on having supporters. The larger your network, the higher your potential leadership.

ᘓ POINT 3 ᘓ
GRATITUDE

As I woke up this Saturday morning, Tom was still asleep. The sun was streaming in, even at 6:30 am in Arizona. I went out on my terrace with the five books I had written before this one.

GRATITUDE BRINGS ANSWERS

As I reviewed the chapter titles, a flood of memories came back to me and gratitude for all the people I've met and experience I've had. Suddenly, thoughts started flooding into me about speeches I could give and ideas for selecting my material.

I'd always dreamed of having a terrace for writing. I thought back to the days when Tom and I were first married, and like many newlyweds, we didn't have two pennies to rub together, let alone a terrace.

That's the funny thing about gratitude. When you use it, things come to you. Things like peace, tranquility, energy, ideas, answers, courage, conviction, joy, and harmony. Even a terrace for writing.

When you have gratitude, people are drawn to you. Things come to you.

GRATITUDE IS THERE, WAITING TO BE NOTICED

When I have moments like today, I wonder why I don't use gratitude more often. There it is, floating - ready to be noticed.

I finished my exercises after Tom went to basketball and as I got up off the carpet, I headed for the air cooler

– it was already 85 degrees. I pressed the switch and felt the cool air.

"Oh, thank you Will," I said out loud, although no one was there to hear me. The cooler had been broken and Will, our all around great at everything handyman, had been over to fix it yesterday.

STOP TODAY AND NOTICE

Then I walked across to the bathroom, and on the way my eye caught the beautiful painting we have on the wall. I see it every day. But today I stopped in front of it. I stood there admiring it as you would in a museum. I glanced at the signature. I'd never paid attention to it before.

"Thank you, Mr. Destordeur," I said again out loud. I thought of the many hours of hard work and talent he had put into that painting, and thought he would like to know I was admiring it, many years later.

YOUR LIGHT, LIGHTS THE WORLD

Gratitude. True gratitude makes your heart tingle. It fills up in your chest, like a light inside. Then, that light in you, radiates to the world.

Several years ago, when my granddaughter was almost three, I took her shopping for shoes. We were bending down on the floor together, buckling each shoe as she tried it on. Suddenly she put tiny arm around my neck and gave me a big squeeze.

AS ADULTS, WE FORGET

No words. Just the squeeze. As children, we have gratitude. As adults, we forget.

The power of gratitude struck me when I was working in the Eastern Block of Europe. Each time I'd cross the border from the post Communist countries to the West, I'd be struck with the beauty and quality we've come to take for granted. Streets that are well paved, grass and trees that are manicured, telephones that work.

IMAGINE WHAT WE TAKE FOR GRANTED

In the post Communist countries when I was there, people had little choice. When they went shopping, it wasn't a matter of looking for clothes they liked. No. There was no selection. No quantity. For them it was a matter of finding anything at all that fit, and the prices were not affordable. Imagine how much we take for granted.

PEOPLE NEED YOUR GRATITUDE

Earlier this morning, my husband decided to call his mother. Our daughter had been visiting there, from across the country, and he wanted to find out how it went. His mother sounded full of joy. She and our daughter, Darrin, had been out shopping for maternity clothes. Darrin and her husband Brad would be proud first time parents in five months. I could visualize the thrill it was for my daughter to shop with her grandmother, for this event in her life.

I told her what was in my heart. "You're such a wonderful grandmother," I said. "I know it means a lot for Darrin to share this special time with you." I looked at my husband. He had tears in his eyes.

BRING JOY TO YOUR LIFE THIS MINUTE

Gratitude. It's everywhere around us – just floating there - ready to be noticed. It's something like a kid, just standing there, waiting for attention. When you give it attention, it brings joy to your life.

Gratitude. If you want to regain the boundless energy and joy of a child, use gratitude in your life every day. Miracles will happen.

•ᔕ POINT 4 ᕪ•
FINANCES

My husband and I had the privilege of meeting Dr. and Mrs. Lyle many years ago. I had won a first class trip to Paris and we traveled across the Atlantic on the SS France. We were in our twenties from California and Dr. and Mrs. Lyle were retired from Texas. They were the most gracious and wonderful role models we could have.

WHATEVER YOU CAN VISUALIZE, YOU CAN CREATE

We learned of Dr. Lyle's financial success and then his loss of everything during the depression. He believed that whatever you can visualize, you can create. He created a dude ranch in Colorado that Tom and I later visited with our three children.

One employee told us that Dr. Lyle wanted to create a lake with fish in it, and everyone said it was impossible.

But Dr. Lyle never gave up. He just kept calling experts until he found one who could do it.

That encounter with Dr. Lyle never left us. Tom and I still believe that whatever *you can envision, you can create.* And I believe you can do, which is why I am writing this book.

What does all this have to do with finance, you might ask!

Dr. Lyle gave us a book he had written called "Preparation for Retirement." Isn't that an odd thing to give a couple in their twenties? We thought so, but Dr. Lyle didn't.

PAY YOURSELF 10% FIRST

He said, "No matter where you are in life, you must start saving 10% for your future. You must pay yourself first before you pay your bills!" 'Impossible,' we thought. We were on a student's income, each working part time, going to school, struggling to make ends meet with three tiny tikes to feed. "No way could we save 10%," we thought.

We came home from that fateful trip and reflected. I said to Tom, "Should we try it for one month?" He agreed. We opened a special account and put 10% into it before the rest went for rent and food.

Do you know what happened? At the end of the month, we had the money in the bank and our lifestyle had not diminished one iota. No one starved. No one had less clothes. We could still buy our student budget, day old doughnuts. We could still go to the movies!

MORE MONEY WON'T HELP

Years later we see that as the turning point. *YOU WILL NOT BECOME FINANCIALLY SECURE BY MAKING MORE MONEY!* This is the biggest fallacy in mankind and womankind. The truth is that most people just spend more when they earn more, and nothing goes to their future.

AVOID CREDIT CARDS

And avoid credit cards, unless you pay them off to a zero balance monthly. One statistic shows that 25% of college students in America have at least $10,000 in credit card debt. This is killing their future. Don't let it happen to you. You must put a percentage away *before* you pay your bills. Little by little it builds.

Because of our savings, we were later able to buy a single rental property, then we sold it and bought a seven unit building.

Later, I had money to start a business, and then I was able to start investing on my own. Years later, our son lived in Hawaii, and on one visit there I saw a rental investment. Tom wasn't interested, so I bought it on my own. I also invest in stocks on my own. Making a joint decision with another person on when to buy and sell is difficult. Each person has his or her own risk comfort level. And you learn best by making your own mistakes.

FINANCIAL FREEDOM NOT IMPRISONMENT

There are two books I suggest reading for inspiration and information. The first is *The Richest Man In Babylon*, by George S. Clason. The second is Suze Orman's book, *The 9 Steps to Financial Freedom*.

DECIDE AND IMPLEMENT

I cannot over-emphasize the importance of this. Until you have financial freedom you will feel imprisoned. What is financial freedom?

You must decide this for yourself. For me it's been having my own bank account from the beginning. It's having my own brokerage account. It's making investment decisions on my own.

What is it for you? You must decide and then implement it.

ESTABLISH CREDIT FOR YOURSELF

When I was 27, I started my first business. It was a shop on the boardwalk in Ocean City, New Jersey. By then, Tom and I were married and had already invested in two rental properties together. I could have used that money for the shop, but I didn't.

Instead I went to the bank. I asked to see the bank manager and I told him I wanted a small loan, just enough for the rent deposit and initial supplies.

Then I paid the loan back with the proceeds of my business within three months. He was delighted, and I had business credit.

I could have taken the money out of our joint account instead of taking the loan. Then I would not have had interest to pay on the loan.

Some people would advocate that route, but that wasn't the route for me. I was happy to pay the interest.

It bought me independence and total responsibility for the success or failure of my business. And it bought me business credit.

Was that right? It was for me.

Now here's the lesson. Throughout your life and career, you'll get a lot of 'expert' financial advice. Should you pay off your mortgage, should you this, should you that? *THERE IS NO RIGHT OR WRONG. There's only what's right for you.*

EDUCATE YOURSELF AND ACT

What is certain though is that you must educate yourself on finances and put money away for your future before you pay your bills. And you must teach your daughters and sons to do it too.

Why do you need a nest egg? Leap ahead to your most desired leadership position. Wouldn't it be nice to have resources to help shape the world?

Could you do it? Yes. Other people have and you can do it too.

GET EXCITED ABOUT YOUR RESOURCES

Here's an example. When I lived in England, it struck me that more needed to be done to encourage young women to go into business. So I started an award program called *The Most Promising Young Businesswoman Award.* It ran for a decade, and over that time we affected a large number of women.

I reasoned that I paid a lot of money in taxes and I didn't necessarily agree with where it all went. So why shouldn't I invest in society in my own way?

It was bold in a way because none of my other friends did such a thing. But once I started the program, the satisfaction was so great nothing could hold me back.

Here's what I did. I designed the application form to make the young women analyze their career choices. If they were short-listed for the award, they attended a special event with speakers and training to stimulate their thinking.

Then finally there was the award winner. All in all, through the entire process, we touched the lives of over 1000 young women.

One of our award winners, Sue Hall said that before she came down to London for the award event, she had never met a woman in business. Since then Sue has gone on become one of the most sought after consultants in her field.

HELP OTHERS TO LEARN

What can you do to help young people start the 10% saving program? Here's what I did with Mayra, a student who came along to help us with this book.

First I explained the concept to her. Then I encouraged her to open a bank account. Lastly, I offered to write two checks for her. One to spend. The other to save. It worked so well that she decided to save 15% instead of 10%!

Yes, you do have the power to influence, and you never know how it will touch another person's life.

YOUR OWN BANKER AND BROKER

Get yourself a banker, one you will know personally. Just walk into a bank and make an appointment. Having your 'own' banker is a powerful feeling. And, having the relationship in advance, helps in times of emergencies.

Have a broker too. You can invest a little or a lot. A good broker will be a great asset. The one I currently use is Scott Gensman of Paine Webber. He uses every day language and is a great networker and supporter of people.

Get your infra-structure in place now. Keep searching and networking until you find the best.

❧ POINT 5 ❧
YOUR ABILITY TO RUN MEETINGS

How often do you go to meetings that start late and ramble endlessly? And, how often do you sit and wait while the meeting runs overtime?

One of the quickest shortcuts to leadership is to become a superb meeting leader! Learn from the ineffective meetings you've attended. Think of all the things you dislike about meetings, and then do it differently.

TIME YOUR AGENDA POINTS

When I took over as Chair of the London Chamber, I felt it was important to end the meetings on time. So when I created an agenda, I marked times next to each agenda point.

I called ahead to each person who was to speak and said, "John, I have 10 minutes allocated for your agenda point. Is that enough?" Invariably they said, "That's fine Christine. I can take even less time if necessary."

GET SUPPORT IN ADVANCE

By getting their support in advance, the meeting runs like clockwork. You can keep your eye on the clock and say, "We have two more minutes on this item. So let's start bringing it to a conclusion."

Try using that technique at your next meeting. It really is effective and makes you a real leadership hero!

GET EVERY MEMBERS INPUT

The second critical factor in leading meetings, is participation from all. In every group there are the 'talkers' and there are the 'listeners.'

I usually find that the 'listeners' have exceptionally good ideas, but are reluctant to speak out. I consider it my job as Chair, to encourage them to contribute.

I go around the table and say, "Mary, what's your idea? Don, what's your idea?" They always have good ideas. Notice I don't say, "Do you have an idea?" I just presume they do, and they do!

By having total participation you'll get the best possible solutions. And the individuals appreciate being acknowledged.

WATCH THE CLOCK

Thirdly, you must keep the meeting on track. Here's how. Don't let people go off on irrelevant tangents, or memory lane. Keep your eye on the clock for each item.

BRING PEOPLE BACK ON TRACK

If someone strays from the subject, use phrases like these to bring them back. "John, can you tell us how your point links to the agenda item first and then fill us in on the detail?"

Use a supportive tone of voice. Or say, "I notice we have two minutes left on this agenda point."

Or, "Perhaps I can summarize what I've heard so far." Then ask the person if it's accurate, and if there's more.

If you need a crutch, write down these types of phrases and keep them in your folder to refer to during meetings. Then you can run the meeting with confidence and effectiveness.

I've had many compliments from Board Members for finishing promptly and keeping meetings on track.

Let's face it, people have busy lives and responsible positions. They don't want meetings to run overtime or to be a waste of time. By honoring people's time, you bring honor to your meeting.

BRING IN A SUPPORTIVE PROFESSIONAL

A very astute businesswoman I know had to Chair her first all male board meeting composed of Directors from four sister companies.

The meeting was expected to be contentious. Although a Chairman is supposed to remain neutral, on this occasion she had a position to protect.

Here's the plan she used. She talked with her accountant ahead of time about the agenda and the points of potential contention.

SHE BECAME THE HERO

At the meeting, his job was to support her with relevant documents and statistics, should it be necessary. The meeting ended at 11 PM and she came out as the hero. She's still chairing that all male board some six years later.

Remember, you can show your leadership talent in running meetings, even if you've never done it before.

Follow these basic principles.

RUNNING EFFECTIVE MEETINGS

1. Put start and finish times on each agenda point.

2. Contact people ahead of time and get their support.

3. Distribute the agenda to each person attending. It's your job to finish each agenda point on time, as well as to start and end the meeting on time.

4. Get all board members to participate by asking for their input.

5. When people go off on tangents, bring them back on track.

6. If you expect contention, bring in a respected professional to support your points during the meeting.

◆ POINT 6 ◆
RELATIONSHIPS – PROFESSIONAL AND PERSONAL

When you think of all the famous Hollywood stars, and all the top corporate leaders, and all the government leaders of the world, there's nothing that makes or breaks success more than relationships.

When I think of my own life experience and of the experience of hundreds of others, I can tell you this. If you master this principle now, you'll reduce your agony, and speed up the road to success.

It will be as if you stepped on an elevator to the 100th floor without stopping, while the others are trudging up the hundred flights of stairs by foot.

Here it is:

You cannot know what is in another person's mind or why they did or said something. You must ask.

NEGATIVE ASSUMPTIONS KILL RELATIONSHIPS

The number one mistake people make is to assume a person meant something by what they said or did, when in fact there was no truth in that assumption.

DON'T WASTE ENERGY FEELING SLIGHTED

An employee of mine suddenly became very sullen. It went on day after day. She never told me her problem.

Finally I asked what was going on. She said she felt slighted that I had not invited her to the scholarship event we were organizing, but had asked her male colleague instead. They had both worked equally hard on the project, and she felt she deserved to go.

My mind, as the boss, was on the event. We were to have 30 young women attending, and I wanted to have a few men present to balance it out. It was as simple as that.

But by not telling me, and assuming I was discriminating against her, she was fostering resentment. She was opening up the floodgates of agony needlessly.

JUST ASK

What could she have done? Just ask. "Christine, I see you asked Paul to go to the scholarship event. Can you tell me why he was chosen?"

The formula is easy. Start using it today every time you feel slighted in some small or large way.

---

3 PART ANTI-CONFLICT FORMULA

1. Don't make assumptions and hold resentment.

2. Go to the offending person and state the case as you see it.

3. Ask why the situation occurred.

John, I see you didn't finish the report last night. Can you tell me about it?

You'll be surprised at the results. Nine times out of 10, the assumptions that were made are wrong.

THERE IS NO PERFECT PERSON

There is no such thing as a perfect person. It's you who must recognize and accept people for what they are, as they are, with blemishes and bruises and capabilities and weaknesses. If you can look at people and situations head on, not with your head in the sand, you'll make your life joyful and successful.

FORGET FANTASY

Don't engage in fantasy. Don't hang your happiness on finding the perfect man, the perfect job, or becoming a mother. Yes, they are all wonderful, but they require work and dedication from your side. It's not like stepping into a wonderland that cures all problems. That's fantasy.

I remember writing to a colleague who was about to get married when I had already been married for seven years. I told her of my belief, that success in marriage was dependent on compromise. And in order to compromise, you must communicate.

4 REASONS FOR FAILURE

Recently I heard Gary Smalley speak. He's a wonderful author on marriage and family subjects. His research shows that the four main reasons for divorce or any relationship split are:

1. Withdrawing from an argument.

I agree with this. If you withdraw, resentment builds and your mind makes the other person an enemy. Usually when my husband and I finish an argument, we discover that we both wanted the same thing. We were just coming at it from different viewpoints. Then we laugh at how much time we wasted by not communicating better before jumping to the conclusion.

2. Escalating the argument.

If you withdraw before you discover this, you'll never make up and will continue to hold resentment.

3. Belittling the other person.

4. Seeing more negatives in the person than there are.

THE SOLUTION IS HONOR

The way to overcome these four points, he says, is to learn to honor the person while arguing or discussing your differences.

Think of that. Each person is on this earth for a reason. If we could honor them completely as we speak to them, our calmness and serenity would open the door for true communication! That's true in business, family and politics.

STOP YOURSELF, STOP OTHERS

By studying and understanding the four points above, you'll be able to recognize them when you see them. If you are guilty of doing any of those four, you must stop.

If someone else is doing it, you must stop them. Usually, people are not doing these things to injure you. They are just copying the role modeling they've had from their parents.

PATTERNS REPEAT THEMSELVES

Here's another important aspect of success in relationships. Watch people's behavior. Are they late, are they disloyal, do they lie, do they speak badly of others? If so, they will do it with you sooner or later. You don't think they will, but they will. You, as a wife or employer, will not turn them into a different person. Only they can do it, and the odds are against it.

Go into business and personal relationships with your eyes open. Once I met a young man who I thought had tremendous potential. He was bright and witty. He had problems at work because he put everyone down and no one liked him. I couldn't understand that. He was so bright and had such potential. I hired him.

Soon he was looking for everything negative he could find in our organization. No client was right, no paperwork was right, no colleague was right. Soon he liked no one, and no one liked him. It was a repeat of his old situation.

NO CRYSTAL BALL NEEDED

It was heartbreaking to see a person of such potential lose out on such a bright future. From this experience I learned to look closely at people's patterns because they will tell you exactly what they will do in their future. You need no crystal ball. Just watch their behavior this minute.

Keep in mind these important facts. One out of eight people have been affected by alcoholism in their family or their close friends.

If the five-year-old son of a drunken alcoholic is picked up by his shirt collar and thrown out the door when he tries to protect his mother from abuse, he'll be deeply affected by it in adulthood. Their reaction to this early life experience, is likely to come up again and again in their relationship with you.

Others grow up with dysfunctional role models and don't know other ways of behavior. Therefore, a large number of people you come in contact with will have varying degrees of dysfunctionality in different areas of their lives which is deeply engrained.

THE CHOICE IS YOURS

Set your standards high. The people you surround yourself with will determine your future. Who do you want as your friend, as your corporate or political supporters, as the father of your children? There are millions of people in the world. The choice is yours. Make it a good one, and your road to success will be smoother, with fewer roadblocks on it. Help your children and your younger colleagues to choose wisely too.

And, last but not least, start today to use the three-part anti-conflict formula above, rather than holding resentment when something goes wrong. Success is in your hands!

◄ POINT 7 ►
PROJECTING YOUR VERBAL IMAGE

Imagine that you're at a meeting and you want to speak out. You have an idea to contribute and you want it to be taken seriously. Perhaps the group is a bit intimidating and you want to have the highest possible credibility.

Here's a way to increase your credibility five fold. In my book and seminar, *Public Speaking and Leadership Building*, I explain the use of 'Credibility Prefaces.'

DON'T DISCREDIT YOURSELF

Here's what not to do. Don't use the 'Discrediting Prefaces' which many people use. Don't say, "I don't know if this is important, but here's my point." That makes your listeners close their ears. Why should they listen to something that's not important? They tune out.

GIVE YOUR STATEMENT MAXIMUM AUTHORITY

Instead, give your statement maximum authority. To do this, give a short credibility statement before your idea. "When I was Chairman of the London Chamber of Commerce, I discovered ..." then give your point. Who wouldn't listen now?

USE PERSONAL CREDIBILITY PREFACES

This draws on your personal credibility. Put your modesty behind you. We're talking about leadership here. We're talking about what you can do to make a difference in your country.

You need to project your credibility in order to make a difference. Go back to Chapter Two and see what leadership or authority positions you've held, or awards you've won. Then have your 'Credibility Preface' ready for the next meeting. You'll see a huge difference.

USE 'CREDIBLE SOURCE' PREFACES

There's another type of 'Credibility Preface' you can use. This one is a credible *source*. Link your idea to something you read in a prestigious magazine or newspaper. "I read in the Wall Street Journal that ..." now give your point. By doing this but you have the credibility of the Wall Street Journal behind you.

USE 'CREDIBLE PERSON' PREFACES

Alternatively you can link your point to a person of high credibility. "When Mary Smith was elected Businesswoman of the Year, she said she supported the project I'm going to tell you about now." Now you have Mary Smith, the Businesswoman of the Year behind you.

What you're doing with these two prefaces is mustering the guns to support your idea. It's not just you and your idea. It has more power.

Easy? Yes. Effective? Yes. Can you do it? Yes. Will you do it? Yes, because you are committed to your future.

What else should you do for high verbal impact? Here are two important to do's. You can apply these instantly and gain high impact.

USE EYE CONTACT

Use good eye contact. A survey was done with a large audience in which the presenter purposely looked at only one half of the audience. What do you think the presenter's rating was with each half? The half that had eye contact gave the speaker a 70% higher rating!

Do you want a 70% higher rating with those you address? Then use eye contact. Use it around the management table, the boardroom table, and even the dinner table. Practice at every opportunity. Entice children, family and friends to practice with you. Your leadership image will go up instantly.

USE CONVICTION

Next, speak with *CONVICTION*. How do you do that? It's not difficult. Just use these two components. Emphasis and pausing.

Read this short phrase: You *have the power*.

Now read it with great voice emphasis on the word power. *You have the POWER*. Good. See how easy that was?

Now say it with a pause before power. *You have the ... power*.

Now say it with pause and emphasize. *You have the ... POWER*.

Isn't that interesting? Look what you achieved with four sentences of practice. Imagine what's possible with constant practice!

Want to go one step further? Use animation. This time deliver the line with pause and emphasis and then pound the table with your fist as you say the word power. *You have the ... power*. Pound table! Wow – look at you! I see you in front of Congress now!

These principles are powerful, yet easy. Practice as you drive. Practice as you walk. Try it on any sentence. You'll be amazed at the impact you'll make.

◆ POINT 8 ◆
<u>VERBAL PERSISTENCE</u>

I met a Councilwoman once and I asked her, "Have you tried calling so and so, as was discussed at the Council meeting?"

She replied, "They usually send their lawyers to everything."

I said, "Yes, that's true, but have you tried to contact them directly?"

She said, "They're always out of town and very hard to reach."

I tried a third time. "But have you actually picked up the phone and tried to reach them yourself?" Their number is in the main document we all have."

Then she said, "No I haven't."

YOU MUST BE ABLE TO GET STRAIGHT ANSWERS

If we want to change society and bring values, we have to be able to get straight answers. You won't want to use this technique on every occasion. But, you must be able to do it when you need to.

Think of all the times that you need to get a straight answer. And yet most people never learn this skill. When you've learned it, you bring enormous personal power to yourself and those you lead.

It's easy with these three steps.

Step 1. Focus on what you're asking.

Step 2. When you get the response, ask yourself if your question has been answered.

Step 3. If not, ask it again.

PRACTICE WITH STRANGERS

Practice with strangers on the phone. The next time you need information from the telephone company or your bank, write your question down before you call.

Then call, and persist until you get your question answered. By doing this, you'll develop this expertise quickly.

If you still don't get a straight answer using this technique, don't get frustrated. It's possibly not your fault. The other person may not think clearly, doesn't know the answer, or doesn't want to give it. You can always go the next level by saying, "Who can tell me the answer to this?"

Try practicing this with a child or a friend. Just ask each other questions and give each other evasive answers.

BE A PRO IN VERBAL PERSISTENCE

Persist in getting straight answers by using the three steps. You'll both come out as pros in verbal persistence.

Your expertise in this will not only help your leadership, but will dramatically reduce your frustration in day to day communication.

◈ POINT 9 ◈
PROJECTING YOUR PHYSICAL IMAGE

I went to court one day to protest a traffic ticket because I thought I was in the right. I dressed professionally so that the judge would view me with more credibility. I wanted everything to be on my side.

While I was waiting for my case to come up, I chatted with a young man who was also there to protest a ticket. He wore jeans and a sloppy T-shirt. He said to me, "I decided to wear this. If the judge doesn't like it, he can lump it."

ONE WINS, ONE LOSES

He lost his case. I won mine. We had practically the same case, but different image projections.

It's said in business, that if we want to be promoted quickly, we should dress the same as those who are one or two steps above us. Whenever my husband comes home from work with his suit on, I'm always surprised at how much more professional he looks than when he changes into his jeans and knit shirt. The same is true for women. If we want to be perceived as leaders, we must dress the part.

Mona Hedstrom learned an important lesson about dress, early in her career, when she attended a conference of about 200 delegates. It was 90% male. "When I attend these types of event I sit in the first row to 'get' everything that's said. The first day I wore a dark blue suit – consulting, conservative," Mona said. "The presenters started with 'Good Morning Gentlemen.' The next day I wore a pink jacket and the presenter started with 'Good Morning – Ladies and

Gentlemen.' I learned that you have to be seen, if you are going to be heard!"

APPROPRIATENESS

Carolyn Miller, the successful image strategist from London, stresses the importance of dressing for the 'appropriateness' of the occasion. We must know which clothes to wear for which event.   Some clothes are appropriate for one occasion but not for another.

Forget about what is comfortable or about your favorite outfit. It's a question of appropriateness. It's a question of leadership.

Think about your wardrobe. You most likely have things that are appropriate for most occasions. It's usually a matter of combining it in a new way. Add a scarf or jewelry. Add a blazer over a blouse. Have a skirt that works for all occasions.

Carolyn says that you don't have to spend a lot of money on clothes. However, spend the larger part of your budget on the clothes you wear next to your face. Those are the picture frames of the face. Wearing earrings, a broach or necklace is like the metals on a uniform. It gives non-verbal credibility.

DRESS ONE LEVEL HIGHER

If you were going to be President of your organization, what would be the ideal outfit to wear to their most formal meeting as their President?

Do you have it? If so, use the technique of dressing one level higher and wear it on that next important occasion. If not, get it and wear it. Dress the part of that position. Soon you'll have it. You've worked hard to get where you are. Don't let yourself down with your image. We need your talent and your leadership.

⋙ POINT 10 ⋙
STAYING FIT

How much influence do you think you have over your physical condition? What good are a great mind and a great bank role without a healthy body?

THE 20 YEAR TEST

Here's an interesting fact. A research report showed that two people can be twenty years different in age and be in the same physical condition. Yes, a 40-year-old can be as fit as some 20-year-olds. And a 65-year-old can be as fit as some 45-year-olds.

PRESERVATIVES POISON

Two components of health are what you put into your body and what you do with your body. In his exceptional book called A *Doctor's Proven New Home Cure for Arthritis*, Dr. Giraud Campbell tells of the dangers of preservatives in food. He shows before and after x-rays of people who stopped consuming preservatives and regained their ability to walk after being bedridden with arthritis.

Imagine then, what preservatives do to our bodies in every way. Each time we eat packaged food, we eat preservatives. Dr. Campbell lists 16 preservatives that are poison to our bodies. These are present in prepared foods, canned foods, bakery goods, pizzas, chocolate, caffeinated drinks, and alcohol. Well, you say, what's left? The answer – natural foods.

PAIN FREE

A friend of mine, Peggy Jessup, told me about Dr. Campbell's book. Her doctor told her that she needed a hip replacement. She heard about this book and decided to follow those principles. Eight months later she had no pain and 20 years later at the age of 80 when she told me the story, she was still pain free and hip replacement free.

Now even with natural foods, we have dangers. We must learn about genetically engineered foods. Are they safe? The US government says they are. Many European countries say they are not, because they alter the cell structure of the food.

TAKE RESPONSIBILITY

The truth is that it's your life and you must take responsibility for it. What about exercise? You don't see it much in schools these days. We recently took our 11-year-old granddaughter Cheryl to a conference with us and the hotel had a fitness center. She loved it. And I have a feeling she always will.

What can you expose your kids to? What kind of role modeling can you do? People who walk every morning say they couldn't live without it.

EXERCISE TOGETHER

I do a 20 minutes exercise every morning that I can do at home or in a hotel when I'm traveling. It includes the five Tibetan rites – Peter Kelder has a book on the subject – and 10 more minutes of either yoga, strength, or endurance building. By doing it immediately upon arising, I make sure it gets done. When my grandchildren come to visit, they often join me. When I travel with other people, we do it together.

I remember having lunch with woman from Santa Barbara, California at a writer's conference. When the dessert came, she said, "No, I won't pollute my temple with that poison!" Tony Robbins said that people, who are thin and fit, train themselves to enjoy the thought of fitness, more than the thought of food.

Take today to reevaluate. Ask yourself this question: 'What condition do I want my body to be in 20 years from now?' What you put in your body in the way of real food, junk food, and chemicals, plus what you do with it today will determine your condition tomorrow.

Use the Tony Robbins system. Let the thought of your fitness be more enticing than the thought of consuming unhealthy foods.

Visualize yourself as the leader you want to be. If you were President of your country or corporation, you would need energy and dynamism. Start on that track now!

7

Saturday

Making It Happen

Chapter Seven

Saturday

Making It Happen

*Change is **not** created by talking
to people who have **no power** to make changes.*

One Wednesday evening, my husband came home from a Neighborhood Association meeting. He was quite upset about something he heard that could evolve into vandalism.

WHAT ACTION HAS BEEN DECIDED UPON?

I asked him what had happened in the meeting. Were other people upset too? Oh yes, they were, in fact several had witnessed the events in question. I asked what action had been decided upon. Were the police going to be called? Was the city council going to be notified?

It was 20 minutes past nine in the evening when I heard the story. I didn't want to take a chance that nothing would be done. I called our neighborhood President to see if he would like support. I suggested that three or four of us call the police and the city council's hotline. He agreed.

I called two others, asked them to call and gave them the number. They agreed to do it. One, to my surprise, had connections with the police force and promised to pass it on.

I called our police sub-station and left a message on their after hours number. I called the main office and requested that police patrol our area the next day. Then I called the hotline.

12 Minutes

That was six phone calls. I looked at the clock. It was 12 minutes since I started. I slept well at night.

The next morning I received two calls backs. The police called to say they had officers on the beat. The neighbor called to say the same thing.

Vandalism never occurred. 12 minutes, six phone calls. I used to not do these things. I used to leave it to others. I used to worry that I would be butting in. I used to worry that the person on the other end of the line would think I had no right to call.

One Phone Call

But I don't anymore. Why? Because I realize this.

We must stop complaining to those around us and start speaking directly to those who have the power to make changes.

Diane Blair was sitting in her car when a man pulled up behind her in a rage and started banging on her car.

She left the scene quickly but reported the offender and his license number to the Sheriff's Department. They subsequently sent an officer to his home to warn him not to do it again.

If we each take a small step, we help society.

ONE GROUP

Mike Landwehr never thought of himself as an activist. Yet 10 years later, with a group of determined colleagues, legislation was changed nationwide so that people with disabilities had the use of public transport, had access to jobs, and were far less segregated.

Think of what's possible when we women unite. *We can turn education around, crime around and values around.*

ONE PERSON

It only takes one person to make a difference. Jacqueline Woods decided that her middle school students were old enough to learn about politics, first hand.

She let them think about the immigration issue of six year old Elian Gonzales, from Cuba. She let them decide how they would handle it if they were in government.

They debated it, came to a consensus, then wrote a letter to Congress and all signed it. They weren't sure about the best way to send it, so they went together to a political party in their city and got assistance in faxing it.

Those children will never forget that they can participate in government.

STUDENTS!

Students can get a jumpstart on leadership by helping society too. Lauren Beth Hickey was first active in the Student Senate, then volunteered for Big Brothers, Big Sisters. In that role, she mentors a 15-year-old teen two to four hours each week. "It makes me feel I give back to society, even while I'm going to college," she says, "and helps another person know they can go to college too."

Lauren also gives her time and talent to Ronald McDonald House that helps families of children who are hospitalized. "I like to bring awareness of the issues to people, and make them see plausible solutions," she says.

OPRAH!

Here's what one man did. His actions raised 11 Million dollars.

The American talk show host, Oprah, featured this man in July 2000. He was of African American decent and his family moved away from the ghetto in his childhood so that he could have a better life.

He returned to the ghetto later to try to help. He went first to the local school. What he found, shocked him. There were no functional school toilets! They were either blocked off or out of order. The kids came to school everyday expecting not to be able to use toilets!

NO DIGNITY

Can you imagine your reaction, if you were expected to go someplace everyday, all day, without access to a toilet? You wouldn't stay there long either, would you?

And what message does that send about dignity? Not the message we want our children and future leaders do have.

This man thought of a way he could change it. He thought back to his Morehouse College studies, and the power of making problems known to those who have the authority to change it.

IT'S STRAIGHT FORWARD

Other people had seen the problem before. Other people had moaned and groaned to each other. But he took action. What he did was straightforward. It was easy enough for ANY of us in society to do.

As you read it, think of your own life and your own community. Where could you apply the basic principle to get similar results?

He drew on the people most affected for support. The kids! Together, a group of 20 or so, equipped themselves with disposable cameras

They photographed the toilets of eight similarly affected schools. They had the photos enlarged – really enlarged for impact. Then they took them to the school board.

11 MILLION DOLLARS

The result?   Eleven   million   dollars   for   school improvement!

When I told that story to Jackie, the thirteen-year-old girl on the plane, she said immediately, "A woman could do that!" Yes she could.

AND THE HOMELESS

I see the problem of the homeless in almost every country I visit. Steve Bacque told me that he supports a charity that takes care of 17,000 homeless people.

The next part is what surprised me. 87% of the 17,000 are women! The majority of them are young, single women with children under the age of seven.

6 MONTHS AWAY

"The average middle class family in America is less than six months from being on the street," says Steve. He emphasizes that we save less, as individuals, than those of any industrialized country. The Japanese do best.

Steve has a rags to riches story himself, and now uses much of his entrepreneurial talent on programs for shelters and the homeless.

BUSINESSPEOPLE CAN HELP AND BENEFIT

Oprah has featured him twice. "I'm trying to let businesspeople see that they can help society and help themselves at the same time," he says. To prove the point he packaged together little dolls that he had made in China, along with a small book of morals and values for kids.

Each doll was hand decorated by the homeless at a piece work rate. Each doll became a guardian angel. A percentage of sales went to Oprah's Angel Work and shelters, and a percentage to Steve's organization, after airing on Oprah's show.

Each side ended up with $750,000 after costs were recouped!

LOOK AROUND YOU

Look around you and see what's evolving. The scandal we had in the White House in 1998, we now have happening among teenagers at lunchtime on school 'playgrounds.'

Our crime rate according to a *Wall Street Journal* report, is the second highest in the world. We have the highest high school drop out rate of any industrialized country.

AMERICA, THE LAND OF FREEDOM AND PROMISE

How does it make us feel to know that America, the land of freedom and promise, has had values, education and crime fall to these levels?

Isn't it time to fix it? People from abroad say that America leads the world. *What direction are we all going?*

The examples in this book come from around the world and let you see that the situation and applications are universal.

THE SITUATION IS UNIVERSAL

The way Hilde Bartlett from England and Janet Lim from Singapore brought bureaucrats to their knees could apply anywhere. You can refer to the index for these sections.

The way Kendall SummerHawk and Pearl Ford-Fyffe handled everyday problems, applies this moment everywhere.

The point is this. Complaining to the wrong person creates no change.

THINK OF THE TEAM BEHIND YOU

Here's what I suggest. Think of all the other people, like those reading this book, who want a better world to live in. Think of them and yourself as one team.

YOU'RE NOT ALONE

When you step up to the plate – when you speak out for change to the people with the authority to change the situation, you're not alone.

Remember that other people are behind you. They are doing it too in their neighborhoods, in their families, with their officials in schools, in crime prevention, in society.

By uniting, we create a national and international conversation that changes the world.

Many people say that the society we have right now is the one we've created. Each of us. We've created it, they say, because of our non-involvement. We've created it by the people we've elected and by not making our voices heard.

BE PROPELLED BY YOUR CONSCIENCE

Always be propelled by your conscience and know that if you don't take action, the problem won't get solved.

Remember this. You do not wake up one morning and suddenly have the courage to walk into the City Council Chambers and address them.

You start as Kendall SummerHawk did, with the little things that can easily be achieved with one phone call.

Your courage and leadership builds as you help society one step at a time.

COMPLAINING TO THE WRONG PEOPLE ... CREATES RESENTMENT

Our time is limited. We can't afford to waste speaking to the wrong people.

What happens if we do? You've seen it millions of times in society, and even in families.

One person sees an injustice. What do they do? Instead of taking it to the person with the power to change it, they come home and complain to their family and friends.

"Oh how awful. Someone should do something." And on and on.

... AND RAGE

What result does that bring? It brings anger. Even rage and resentment.

... AND CANCER IN SOCIETY

Dr. Simonton, the cancer recovery specialist from Texas, says that resentment is the biggest cause of cancer. Right now our societies are cancer ridden.

Every step that you take to fix something, small or large, helps to rid the cancer and bring values, pride and dignity to society.

PROBLEM – ACTION – LEADERSHIP

Decide now. What is your passion? What is the problem you want to devote yourself to?

Will you join a group or go it alone? Can you raise your leadership abilities at the same time?

PREACHING TO THE CONVERTED?

If you find a group, assess for yourself whether or not they really get action. Before you join, see if they dissipate their energy through inner politics or preaching to the converted.

3 QUESTIONS TO ASK BEFORE JOINING AN ORGANIZATION

1. Does this organization really get results from their actions, or are they preaching to the converted?

2. Will my involvement increase my leadership ability?

3. Will my time and energy here help to improve education, reduce crime or achieve results for society in the area of my concern?

If the answer to all three is yes, by all means join. Throw yourself into it and join their leadership.

If you observe their organization and see that the answer is no to ANY of the three questions, you have two choices.

1. Find another group.

2. Activate change on your own.

WHAT ACTION WILL YOU TAKE TODAY WHEN YOU SEE A PROBLEM?

The Eiffel Tower incident only took us about 20 minutes of our time.

The neighborhood incident against vandalism only took 12 minutes.

HERE'S A QUESTION

Now let me ask you this question. What if all of us, all at once, did a turn around? What if all of us started calling it as it is.

What would that look like? I see it like this. I see a reversal happening almost instantly.

I see people being willing to take one or two minutes out of their lives to pick up the phone to make a call for action.

The people of Sacramento did it. They didn't look the other way when the student broke the law by engaging in indecent exposure at graduation. *They called the school and spoke out for values.*

THE EMPEROR HAS NO CLOTHES

Women of the world unite. It's time stop playing *The Emperor Has No Clothes.* The problems are here and we, the average citizens, must start speaking out to the right people to get them fixed.

IT CAN HAPPEN QUICKLY

Think of what we can accomplish quickly when we women unite. Education can be pride worthy again, crime can be reduced, and values can be restored again.

So what will cross your path today? A wrong that needs to be righted? Whatever it is, pick up the phone and make the call.

And perhaps you'll want to start a focus group for *Can a Girl Run For President?* as Sue Dyer suggests in the

Foreword. You can contact us through my website for support.

YOUR CREDIBILITY WILL GROW

As you experience the changes that occur *because of your action*, your credibility will grow. Your experience will grow. Your actions will be faster and better. And the synergy of action from people around you will grow.

Use the stories in this book to help you reflect on your credibility, and to remind you of your vision.

As you review a chapter each day, let the stories inspire you. Let the methods become part of your daily routine.

Start today with the very thing that crosses your path. Don't wait for others. I know that you'll make a difference. You have the power within you to influence your world around you.

Remember, your self-development will take you to new levels of leadership and personal satisfaction you never dreamed possible.

Wishing you the best in your ventures,

Christine Harvey
Tucson, Arizona and
London, England

ChristineHarvey@Compuserve.com
www.ChristineHarvey.com

Appendix 1: Keynote Speech

By
Christine Harvey

to the
Leaders of the North Atlantic
Girl Scouts of America

In Garmisch Germany, March 25, 2000

Fellow Americans, and Distinguished Guests from all over the world,

I want to start by asking you a question: Can a girl run for President? Can a girl run for PRESIDENT of the United States? But wait, wait!

Before you answer,,, Can a girl run for President – not from YOUR eyes, not from MY eyes, not from your neighbor's eyes – because that's not the important thing. The question is, Can a girl run for President from the eyes of a 10 year old?

I want you to think about how important women are decision making. You know...everything from designing kitchens to running governments. Women all over the world ask me why I think we don't have more women in decision making positions. So I started to analyze it.

One of the things I noticed that was holding women back in conferences and public meetings was that they didn't speak out enough in big groups. So men got more of the limelight and leadership credit.

I thought, "What shall we do about it?" So I got a group of four powerful female speakers together in different parts of the nation and I said, "Let's teach YOUNG girls how to speak out and have INFLUENCE – say ... ages 9 to 11."

Let's give them public speaking tools *before* they hit the self conscious age. They may hold onto these skills and confidence forever. That will increase female leadership in the world . So I organized a group of girl scouts, ages 9 to 11, from girl scouts and designed a really lively program for them. I had them *jumping* out of their chairs - giving speeches about their vacations – using eye contact. After each speech, all of them gave positive feedback to each other. WOW. THEY WERE TERRIFIC.

The best part came last, when I asked them how they'd use their new influence skills. One girl wanted to be a veterinarian when she grew up. I'll never forget her. A petite little gal. She said, "I'm going to use these speaking skills to change legislation involving animals."

I thought, "How incredible...*changing legislation!* This is getting better results than I imagined!" Then came the last girl. SHE got up and said, "I'm going to run for Class President tomorrow and I'm going to use these skills to get elected!"

"What timing," I thought. I was SO thrilled was thinking, "This one's going to grow up and be a Vet and change legislation... Hallelujah... That one's going to run for Class President – fantastic – we are on a roll. This generation is not even going to know what a glass ceiling is!"

But the next day the bubble burst. My friend, the Troop Leader said to me, "Christine, you'll never guess what happened in Miss Smith's 4th grade class! A little ten year old girl, who was NOT at our training, put up her hand and said timidly, "Miss Smith, can a GIRL run for President of the United States?"

My heart sank to the floor. Can a girl run for President!!!! I thought, "This is the dawn of the millennium. A chill ran through my spine. We think we've come so far, ..SO FAR"

Can a girl run for President. You see, that little 10 year old girl had never seen one before. She'd never seen a woman in that position before and she wondered ....Can a girl BE President?

And why is that so important to her? And this point is critical. It's because at age 10 she's asking herself, "Where should I set *MY* limits?" Her mind is racing – "After all, if I can't be President...what else *CAN'T* be? ... What do I dare to *DREAM?* better just not try, you see. I'd better *JUST...NOT...DREAM.*

You see, when she's asking that question, 'Can a girl run for President,' she's actually asking about her own life. Her mind is thinking, "Teacher, teacher, what CAN I do? Teacher, teacher, what can I dream? If a girl can't be President, where should I set my limits?... How do I value myself?"

And that, Ladies and Gentlemen, is why I'm here to speak to you tonight.

What *messages* are your girls getting? What messages are your girls getting from society...from family ...from you...from me?

Are your girls limiting themselves from these messages? I hope not – because the *world needs them* operating at their highest potential.

Let me show you what I mean. Two years ago, I went going to Bosnia to tape a TV special called "The Heart and Soul of Leadership." Before the trip, I interviewed dozens people, and I chose Colonel Julie Manta, a female Colonel in Bosnia. I wanted the ones who could express the highest integrity. She was still in her 30's and was in command of 1200 troops.

I asked her what guiding principle allowed her to move up the ladder so quickly. Here's what she told me. She said, "Christine, I teach my people that we must not lie, cheat or steal, or *TOLERATE* those who do. ..Or *TOLERATE* those who do.

I'll never forget my reaction to that. All my life I believed we should not lie, cheat or steal. But when she said we should not *TOLERATE* those who do, it hit me like a thunder bolt.

Yes! Think of what a different SOCIETY we would have if we stopped TOLERATING those who do!

And what messages are girls *still* getting FROM society? Recently, I was miniature golfing with my seven-year-old grandson. We overheard a man on the golf course say "Give her another chance – she's just a girl."

"Give her *another chance* - she's just a girl." People use these expressions in jest. They don't realize they are LIMITING the self image of young girls, AND perpetuating a destructive myth. They don't realize they are *STEALING* the leadership image of women and *THEREBY...LIMITING...SOCIETY.*

I still hear remarks about 'woman drivers'. My own father was visiting two weeks ago. He made a remark about the 'woman driver' in the car ahead. Something like, 'What do you expect? She's just a woman.' My father is 82. I've always let it slide by before...I always thought, "What's the difference!"

But that time, I thought of my granddaughter who was 10. So I said to my Dad...with compassion...not anger. "Dad, you *know* that women drive as well as men these days. I don't want my grandchildren to hear demeaning language like that." To my surprise, he didn't complain and he hasn't done it since.

People don't realize that when they limit the potential of others, *or themselves,* they are stealing a resource from the world. We must not let this language slide by. We must not let this believe system slide by.

Can a girl be President? Yes, but first we have to stop people from saying such things as 'She's *JUST* a girl.'

Right now in society, we need the BEST leadership we can get.

And I believe, that *we are sitting on a Gold Mine*. That Gold Mine of girls is *right in front of you* each week. And YOU are the stewards of that Gold Mine.

Right now in society, we need values and excellence in leadership. Leaders of society who won't settle for second best. And who better to provide it than our Gold Mine?

It's been predicted that the new millennium will be the age of female leadership. But IF that's going to be true, our girls need to learn to *SPEAK OUT* for the values they believe in. They need to learn to do it
now, and they need your help.

Why? Let's look at education ...The Wall Street Journal reported that the high school drop out rate in the United States is ... *twenty eight percent*...28%. That's the average. That means that in some places it's EVEN higher. Now ... how high is 28%? It's the *HIGHEST* of *ANY* ...industrialized nation.

Fellow Americans and friends, how long are we going to tolerate that? Are our children less intelligent than those in 21 other top nations? NO. But the *system* needs values and excellence in leadership.

That was the drop out rate. What about subject ranking. Science? We ranked 16th. Math? We ranked 19th. statistics from the Wall Street Journal.

We need leaders who won't settle for second best... who won't tolerate having us in last place. Who will speak out to cure these ills of education? Who will take on the values driven leadership in this millennium? The answer – Our Gold Mine. Our Gold Mine in front of you each week!

Here's another challenge we need help on...that's *crime*. Since 1971, the prison population, has increased, *six-fold*. We now have the largest percentage of citizens behind bars than every country except one.

My fellow citizens, how long will we *tolerate* that? I spoke to someone who visited a prison last year. He said the drug dealers in prison there had cell phones. They continued to run their drug trade from *prison*. Not only that, but they paid *other* inmates to do their prison duties for them, so that they had more time to run their drug trade from prison.

Why, are we tolerating that? Who will speak out to cure the ills of crime? Who will take on the values and excellence in leadership in this millennium? The answer – the gold mine in front of you each week at your Girl Scout meeting.

And what about the future? Technology. Innovation. There are many exciting, but controversial issues on our horizon. Issues which are even deeper than education and crime. Issues like genetically engineered foods. The Europeans say it's not safe for our human bodies. Our government officials say it is safe. Who do we trust? Do we know enough about it to decide? Or are we putting blind faith into our officials?

And cloning. If it goes any further, who will provide the value driven leadership to guide the future of society?

What's my message here? We *NEED* those girls in leadership so that we can use 100% of our human resources. *Men AND Women*. We have... *tough*... challenges.

What's the answer? The Gold Mine of girls in front of you each week. But our girls have to be trained. First to spot the problem. Second to speak out, and third to speak out to the *right* people. And that's where you come in, the stewards of the gold mine, to teach them to *think* of themselves as leaders of values and excellence...*AND*...as future Presidents.

Here are the three training steps again for creating leaders which values from that Gold Mine of girls (and women) 1. Spot the problem 2. Speak out, 3. Speak out to the *right* people.

Here's an example of what I mean. Three summers ago I was in Paris with a friend for a conference. We arrived early and decided to go to the Eiffel Tower. I have a bit of height fright, so I bought a ticket, which allowed me to go to levels one *and* two.

I wanted to go to level one first, to see how I liked it. But the guard wanted me to go to level two first. When we tried to explain what we wanted, he started to shout at us and then he took his hands, and physically shoved us a distance of five feet.

We then went to another guard who let us go to level one. I said to my friend, "Well, there's an example of verbal abuse if I ever saw one." My friend said, "Yes, *AND* it was also physical abuse."

"Gosh, you're right," I said. I was so focused on the verbal abuse that the physical hadn't registered. And so that's what I mean by noticing. If you don't recognize the ills of society, you can't fix them.

So, we went up the elevator by the new gardened had a lovely time. As we were walking out, we were tempted to forget the whole thing. But I said to my friend Hilde, "I guess we'd better report this so that the guard doesn't abuse other tourists. Anyway, it's not good for the public relations of the country to have him in that position."

She agreed. So we went to office of the Managing Director at the foot of the Tower. He wasn't in so we calmly wrote a letter by hand and signed it. After my name I wrote my Title,

Past Chairman, London Chamber of Commerce. My friend signed it and wrote her Title, Business Women of the Year.

We photocopied the letter and kept a copy. After a week we had no answer, so we typed it and we mailed it. An apologetic letter came back saying that it was not the guard's first offense and that he would go to a tribunal for judgment.

Two weeks later the world press was in a stir. The Eiffel Tower was closed temporarily because the guard was fired and the union members went on strike to protest. As the newspapers said, our action prevented others from abuse.

Now, in reflection, here's the important thing. Did we get angry and let it spoil our trip? No. Did we complain to the guards? No. They were not the right people to complain to, because they had no authority to create change. Did we waste our energy complaining to each other or our friends back home? No. That 's a displaced use of energy.

The critical difference is that we spoke out to the top person - the one with the power to create change, and that's step 2 and 3. SPEAK OUT and speak out to the RIGHT person – the person who can create change. And we must *train* ourselves and others to DO it.

Here's another example. My same friend Hilde and I were having dinner together, near my house by Brussels where I lived at the time, when her purse was stolen. When we went to the Police Station to file the report, the desk clerk refused to take the report. She said, "There's nothing that can be done, so why bother." We insisted for 20 minutes and finally she let us file the report.

Then we said, "We SAW the thieves and we can identify their photographs." She said, "Oh no, you can't identify photos NOW! You'll have to come back Monday morning." We said "Why should other people be at risk all weekend?" She finally let us go up to the third floor to the *chief* of the Crime Squad.

He was *delighted* to meet us, and thrilled that we cared. We identified the photos. The crime ring was arrested and sent back to their home country.

The Crime Squad Chief was SO pleased that he sent us home with a squad car that night, because the keys to my apartment were in the stolen purse. An hour after we got home, the doorbell rang. Do you know who it was? The Crime Squad Chief, stopping by to thank us!

Speak out. And speak out to the *right* person.

Education, crime, direction of innovation – just three of the hundreds of areas in which we need values and excellence in leadership now and in the future.

I'd like you to think for a moment, now, of each girl around you. In other words, think of... *A L L*... the nuggets in your gold mine of girls around you. Let one of them come to mind. Imagine writing down her name. Now think to yourself, 'If I knew that someday THAT young women would be the leader of our country... someday she would be PRESIDENT what must I teach her now? Imagine what you would do differently.

How should you treat her? How must you train her, to treat others with dignity?

And then think of her again. When she speaks, how will you *L I S T E N* ? Usually we superficially listen to kids. But to create leaders, to give them dignity and *belief* in themselves, we have to *L I S T E N*. Listen with our heart, listen to understand, listen to share their *feelings*. This gives credibility to them *AND* to their ideas. Not the 'in one ear and out the other' type of non-listening they often get from others.

Now think of your gold mine again. Let another girl come to mind - Imagine writing down HER name - this one our future Vice President? Think of value driven leadership. What would you teach her? How would you treat her and train her to treat others? How would you prepare her to speak out, to listen to needs of others, to create win-win situations? Imagine writing down what you would do differently?

Now think of all the girls around you again. Pick one for Secretary of State, one for Secretary of Defense, Treasury. Who will you have to head up education for your state, the prison system, the Medical Association, the Legal Association.

When you see them, think of all those nuggets in your gold mine as *HEADS* of government, *HEADS* of corporations. Use the language you would use with those future leaders. Use the training and the *DIGNITY* you would use, to create *VALUE ..DRIVEN ...LEADERS*.

Train them to speak in public, to use eye contact, to give each other positive feedback. *1   I'll give you support on it. That's what this pink sheet is. Everything you need is on here. For 10 girls, it will take you about an hour and a half. It's a short investment, with a big return. You'll get that sheet at the door when you leave.

Also stop young women when they use words that limit their own self esteem and dignity. Stop others when they use negative words and images. Stop *ANYONE* who says, "She's *JUST* a girl." Remember that verbal abuse for girls, done in jest, is still verbal abuse. It limits society because it blocks their future leadership. Don't ... tolerate it. *Talk* to them, like I talked to my Dad. Not with anger, but with compassion.

When you go back to your girls, think of your role as stewards of the future. It's said that when government officials get as few as five letters on an issue, *they take notice.*

When you train your girls to write to their congressmen and women, let them sign their names, and under it, let them write their titles. Instead of Past Chairman of the Chamber of Commerce or Past Business Woman of the Year, let them be *FUTURE* Chairman, *FUTURE* Businesswoman, Future Leader of America. This *will* get attention from their government officials. They will get answers.

When the girls sign their future titles, it will *impact* their psyches. It will put them on a new leadership plain ... for their *entire* lives. All action, all success... is *prefaced* by belief.

Help them think of issues that matter. Let them think of solutions. Kids are smart. Help them think of appropriate avenues to speak out. It might be a letter to a Senator. Or it might be a phone call to a talk show. It might be a meeting with the Principal or a Corporate President.

Kids are impressionable. You don't need to do it over and over. Once is enough. They'll never forget. When I was young, my Girl Scout leader taught us to make a camp mat out of old newspapers to stay warm. We made a stove out of a tuna can. I was so amazed. I was so proud. It marked MY psyche.

Do you know the message I got? The message from that simple tuna can heater? Self sufficiency. Yes, I said to myself at that tender age, if I can do this, I can take care of myself *anywhere*. Self sufficiency. Since then I've started three businesses of my own, I've traveled alone to India and Egypt and 20 other countries. Self-sufficiency does NOT turn girls into loners. I'm still married to the man I married in 1961. We have three children and two grandchildren.

When I started my career, I heard a psychologist say, "Woman *can* have their cake and eat it too – marriage, family *and* career. Men have been doing it for centuries." That made me think of my life differently, and to let myself have more possibilities.

Your actions, as a Girl Scout leader, will mark the psyche of your girls too. TIME IS SHORT. Values and excellence in leadership is needed *now*. The future is in your hands and I *know* you will make an impact.

Before I end, I'd like each of you to reflect on one important action you can take, when you get back. Take a moment to think now. What will you do? Imagine writing it down. Now think of another action. What is that? Imagine writing that down. Make a commitment *now*, to do *at least* those two things. And, I would be very pleased if you would come up afterwards and tell me what they are.

I also invite you do contact me by E-mail for support on any of these points. Perhaps we can form a group to implement a nationwide speaking and influence program for girls, as I talked about earlier. It could be a video based training, which anyone could use with girls anywhere, anytime...with their troop, or their class, or their neighborhood. So easy.

My e-mail address is ChristineHarvey@compuserve.com. And I ask you to keep this address for a special reason. Besides being able to email me to tell me that YOUR girl has become President, you'll be able to tell generations to come.

I know there is a lot to refer back to, so we've organized copies of this speech in print and audio format for you. I hope that's helpful. You'll receive the written text at the door and the audio by mail.

Can a girl run for President? Can a girl BE President? Can a girl provide the value driven leadership we need? The answer is Yes. But only with you as the spearheads.

Since 1912 Girl Scouts has helped over 43 million girls to develop their potential. In a survey done of 54 top women of distinction in America, 84% of them cited Girl Scouts as impacting their lives and their careers. The probability that the first female President of the United States will come from Girl Scouts, is right here in these statistics.

Now, my friends, it's time for your impact on your girls. You 250 in this room, represent over 6500 Girl Scouts. It would take a room 25 times this size, to hold that many. Look around the room. Visualize these 6500 girls represented here, and realize that someday at least one will be President of our United States. Others will be Secretary of State, Secretary of Defense, and Corporate Presidents. Make sure they are all value driven leaders of all walks of life, family, and community.

I ask you to look around the room again at the 250 other stewards of our Gold Mines... We have leaders.. I'll call you the 'front line stewards'. We have the trainers and ALL others in this room...I'll call 'supporting stewards" Now I want you to do me a favor. You'll need your hands free and your laps free. Are you ready?

Stand up if you're a leader....... Thank you!

Stand up if you're a supporter of the leaders. That's everyone else in the room....... Thank you!

Now, anyone...... *STAND UP IF YOU BELIEVE A GIRL CAN BE PRESIDENT!!* ....Thank You!!!

PROMISE yourself, that you will look at your Gold Mine through new eyes. Promise yourself that you'll teach them to *NOTICE* what needs changing, to *SPEAK OUT*, and to speak out to the *RIGHT* people.

When you do this, I promise you, that the world will be a better place and *YOU*, each one of you, will have been the driving force!

The End

Copies of the speech are available in audio and video format

Appendix 2: Girls Speaking Program

Designed for Self Confidence, Esteem Building and Leadership

This One Day Program for young girls is extremely powerful. You do NOT have to have public speaking experience to run it. Simply follow the guidelines below and have a wonderful time. The ideal age is approximately 9 to12 years. Good Luck. Write to us via our website or email to let us know your experience, or ask questions.

1. SET-UP
    Set up chairs in rows before the girls arrive.

2. OPENING
    (A)   Open program by asking the girls if they ever have to influence anyone, for example, their parents (to let them go to the movies) or their teachers or their friends.
    (B)   Tell them that that these speaking and influence skills will help them forever and that they will never forget them.

3. DEMONSTRATE EYE CONTACT (WRONG/RIGHT)
    (A)   Demonstrate the wrong and right way by doing eye contact as you talk for a few seconds about your favorite vacation for one minute.
    Wrong = look down at floor and pace back and forth as you talk.
    Right = stand still and look into the eyes of each girl as you talk about your favorite vacation.

4. EXPLAIN THE PROGRAM
    Tell them that they'll each have one minute to talk about their favorite vacation.

5. EXPLAIN POSITIVE FEEDBACK
    (A)   Teach positive feedback.
    Say to the girls, "You have two important roles here today. One is speaking. But the most

important is listening and watching to each girl as she speaks, so that you can pick out one thing you like."

(B)   Demonstrate positive feedback

Say here's an example: 'Suzie I like your eye contact and the way you pointed out the window when you talked about the mountain'.

Say, "After each speaker finishes, each of you will give her your positive feedback."

6   FIRST GIRL SPEAKS

(A)   Choose the first speaker who will stand in front of the group and talk about her vacation.

(B)   Tips:

1. Do not criticize or instruct her.

2. Start with the 3 or 4 most outgoing girls - this gets the ball rolling favorably.

(C)   Time 60 seconds, then start clapping. That's the signal that her time is over. Have all the girls join you in clapping (if a girl finishes early that is fine, start clapping.)

The task is to build confidence and make it a favorable experience, even if she talks for a shorter period.

7.   FIRST GIRL GETS POSITIVE FEEDBACK

(A)   Let her remain standing while YOU tell her one thing you liked.

(B)   Then have each girl give one thing they liked. It is O.K. to repeat what another person liked. Each girl should give positive feedback even if it's the same as another girl's feedback.

8.   SECOND GIRL SPEAKS

9.   SECOND GIRL GETS POSITIVE FEEDBACK

10. REPEAT CYCLE UNTIL FINISHED (SPEAK/POSITIVE FEEDBACK)

11 CONGRATULATE ALL OF THEM

(A)   Keep your enthusiasm high.

(B)   Remember you are NOT teaching them to speak, rather your role is to keep enthusiasm high and to facilitate positive feedback.

12. EACH GIRL TELLS USAGE

(A)   Have each girl stand in front of the group and tell how they will use these skills in the future (this is a vital part of the program, don't skip it.)

(B)   Congratulate each one and make a positive comment on how useful that will be to them.

TIME REQUIRED

Opening = 1 minute:

Demonstrate eye contact = 1 minute:

Explain program and positive feedback = 1 minute.

Speaking = 60 seconds per girl to speak, plus positive feedback, about 30 seconds per girl:

Each girl tells how she will use the skills in the future - 1 minute

Total time for 10 girls = about 1 1/2hour.

Appendix 3: Resources

❦❦❦❦❦❦❦

Organizations

Big Brothers, Big Sisters
Check website:
www.bbbsa.org for local
BBBS information or
similar organizations.
Links young people
approximate age 7-18 with
older mentors for moral
support.

Dale Carnegie Training
Tel. 1-888-966-8379
Award winning courses in
communication skills and
public speaking.

Girls Incorporated
120 Wall Street
New York, NY 10015
Tel. 1-212-509-2000
Fax. 1-212-502-8708

Girl Scouts of the USA
420 Fifth Ave.
New York, NY 10018
Tel. 1-800-478-7248

Junior League
Check your local directory

League of Women Voters
1730 M Street NW
Washington, DC 20036
Tel. 1-202-429-1965
Fax. 1-202-429-0854
75300.3121@compuservecom
www.lwv.org

NAWBO
1411 K Street NW
Washington, DC 20005
Tel 1-800-556-2926
www.nawbo.org

NOW – National Organization For Women
1000 Sixteenth St. NW
#700
Washington, DC 20036
Tel. 1-202-331-0066
now@now.org.
www.now.org

RFW-Resources For Business
Tel. 1-520-881-4506
rfwtucson@aol.com
www.tucson.com/rfw

The Heart of America Foundation
201 Massachusetts Ave. NE #C5
Washington, DC 20002
Tel. 1-202-546-3256
Fax. 1-202-546-3237
heartofam@aol.com
www.heartofamerica.org

The Oprah Magazine
P.O. Box 7831
Red Oak, IA 51591
www.ccare.hearsomags.com

Toastmasters International
Tel. 1-800-993-7732
www.toastmasters.org
World's largest international organization helping men and women improve their public speaking and communication skills.

YWCA of the U.S.A.
Empire State Building
350 Fifth Ave. Suite 301
New York, NY 10118
Tel. 1-212-273-7800
Fax. 1-212-465-2281
www.ywca.org

Zonta International
557 West Randolph St.
Chicago, IL 60661
Tel. 1-312-930-5848
Fax. 1-312-930-0951

Access to 9000 Womens Groups
www.electrapages.com

International Training & Consulting (ITC)
2761 N. Country Club Rd.
Tucson, AZ 85716
Tel. 1-520-323-0495
Fax. 1-520-323-4586
ITC helps countries in development or transition to obtain skills and knowledge necessary to function in the world economy.

Democratic National Committee
430 S. Capitol St. SE
Washington, DC 20003
Tel. 1-202-863-8000

Republican National Committee
310 First St. SE
Washington, DC 20003
Tel. 1-202-863-8500
Fax. 1-202-863-8820
info@rnc.org

Libertarian National Committee
1-800-682-1776

Natural Law Party
P.O. Box 1900
Fairfield, IA 52556
Tel. 1-800-332-0000
Political alternative for
sustainable solutions and
new direction.
www.natural-law.org
info@natural-law.org

Young Republicans
webmaster@ym.org

Young Democrats
yda@dnc.democrats.org

◄۶◄۶◄۶◄۶◄۶◄۶◄۶

Individuals and Their Companies

Mike Adubato
European Toastmasters,
Belgium
Pee-Wee Soccer Coach
adubato@skynet.be

Steve Bacque
Business and
Entrepreneurial
Institute of North America
Tel. 1-908-925-8383
Fax. 1-908-925-9090
sbacque@bellatlantic.net
www.beina.netcom

Hilde Bartlett
Silicon Valley Group, PLC
England
Tel. 44 (0) 1-276-455-900
Fax. 44 (0) 1-276-455-910
hilde.bartlett@silicon-
valley.co.uk
www.silicon-valley.co.uk

Irena Belohorsha
Parliament of Slovakia

Diane Blair
It Fits!/BBB Bed &
Breakfast
Tel. 1-520-744-8770
ItFits@bbbtucson.com

Henry Blount
President of Paris/Brussels
Chapter of Professional
Speakers Association

Deborah Chah
Country Club Homes
Tucson, Arizona
Tel. 1-520-741-0477

Louise Clymer
Louise Clymer Tax and
Accounting
Tel. 1-520-290-6099
mlclymer2@aol.com

Eva Doyle
Psychologist/Therapist/
Professional Speaker
Brussels, Belgium

Silvija Dreimane
Parliament of Latvia

Sue Dyer
OrgMetrics
Livermore, California
1-925-449-8300
www.orgmet.com

Nancy Faville
RFW-Resources For
Business
Tel. 1-520-881-4506
rfwtucson@aol.com
www.tucson.com/rfw

Ingrid Flory
Flory Consulting
Lobbying for packaging
industry, particularly on
environmental issues.
and
Regemus Co.
Tel. (46-08) 7171-0505
Fax. (46-08) 717-0545
'Boardmanship,' lecturing on
how to run efficient Boards,
advantages of boards to
small and medium size
companies, how to deal with
entrepreneurial family
companies, plus specific
training for women
interested in Board work.

Pearl Ford-Fyffe
InfoFax – RFW-Resources
for Business Network
Connection and Avon
Products, Inc.
pearlff@flash.net

Scott Gensman
Paine Webber
Tel. 1-520-750-7500
Fax. 1-520-750-0589

Kim Green
Veritas Communications
1-520-529-1007

Gail Grossetta
Grossetta International
LLC
Tel. 1-520-298-8898
Fax. 1-520-298-9689

Lou Heckler
Professional Speaker and
Trainer
LouHeckler@aol.com

Mona Hedstrom
Information Technology
Professional/Past President
of several women's networks
Frankfurt, Germany
Tel. 49 69-67-6313

Sharon Hekman
Arizona-Kazakhstan
Partnership Foundation
Tucson, Arizona
Tel. 1-520-327-1904

MJ Jensen
IdeaMagic marketing &
promotions
1-520-751-4906
www.ideamagic.com

Connie Kadansky
8725 N. 6th Drive
Phoenix, AZ 85021
Tel. 1-602-997-1101
Fax. 1-602-678-0754
www.exceptionalsales.com

Diane Katz, Ph.D.
Harmony, LLC
Tel. 1-520-544-0687
dkharmony@aol.com

Nancy Thompson
Kiernan, Ph.D.
azgato@aol.com

Carol Larson
Good Works
Tel. 1-480-964-1125
Fax. 1-480-964-0555

Janet Lim
Borneo (Toyota) Motors
Private Limited
Singapore
dtakelly@pacific.net.sg

Paula Maxwell
Republican Headquarters
Tucson, Arizona
Tel. 1-520-321-1492

Barbara Mintzer
Professional Speaker
bmntzer@west.net

Lisa Nutt
Instructor, Pima
Community College
Tucson, Arizona

Alain Petillot
European Toastmasters,
France
apetillot@free.fr

Donna Reed
Tools For Achievers, Inc.
1-520-299-8199
toolsach@aol.com

Elaine Richardson
Arizona State Senator

Richard Rodgers
Senior Minister,
Unity of Phoenix
Rogers@goodnet.com

Gary Smalley
Author of "For Better or For
Best" and "Making Love
Last Forever."

Pam Smith
Re-Design Interior
Rearrangement
1-520-886-8060
pamsmith@aol.com

Ruth Smith
RKS Mortgage and
Financial Business
Consulting
rks@vbe.com

Kendall SummerHawk
Heart of Success
1-520-577-6404

Beth Walkup
BethofTucson@aol.com

Reesa Woolf, Ph.D.
Executive Public
Speaking Coach
1-973-335-7361
rwwoolf@ix.netcom.com
www.accentonpublicspeaking.com

Emergency Phone Numbers

National Domestic
Violence Hotline
1-800-333-7233

I Wish the Hitting
Would Stop
1-800-627-3675

National Council Child
Abuse
1-800-222-2000

Youth Crisis Hotline
1-800-422-4673

Al-Anon Family Group
Headquarters
1-800-356-9996

Alcohol & Drug Abuse
Help
1-800-252-6465

"Just Say No"
International
1-800-258-2766

National Crime
Prevention Council
1-800-937-7383

Mothers Against Drunk
Driving
1-800-777-6233

Crime Stoppers
1-800-252-8477

Index

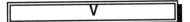

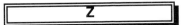

BOOKS AND TAPES BY CHRISTINE HARVEY

Can A Girl Run For President?
Use the world as your arena as you develop your leadership. Step-by-step methods and advice for getting to the top by women around the world. Overcome limitations and reach your full potential. $14.95

Secret's of the World's Top Sales Performers
Ten people in 10 industries in 10 countries give you unique perspectives that can easily be adapted to your needs. A must for sales and non-sales people alike. 150,000 copies in 5 languages. $6.95

Your Pursuit of Profit: Christine Harvey with Bill Sykes
If you are in management, sales, run your own company, or simply want to advance, this book will help you. Pointers from hundreds of industries worldwide. 140,000 copies—8 languages. $14.95

Successful Selling
Looking for a new way to handle objections and closings? Would self-motivation and support systems really keep you going? Proven answers to these and other roadblocks. In 12 languages. $6.95

Successful Motivation
Do you want to motivate yourself and others to new levels? Seven methods for dealing with situations from difficult people to procrastination to raising productivity and job performance. $14.95

Public Speaking and Leadership Building
Pick this book up and use the methods today. Every situation for the beginner and the pro. Increase your ability step-by-step as your fears dissolve. In 5 languages. Workbook format. $89.95

Power Talk
Video or Audio
Powerful speaking and leadership techniques.
V – $39.95 / A – $14.95

Can A Girl Run For President?
Video or Audio
Christine Harvey's speech to American GS Leaders of Europe.
V – $39.95 / A – $14.95

3 Steps to Business and Personal Success – Audio
Interview with top sales performer Janet Lim, and a motivating speech about the Secrets of the World's Top Sales Performers. $14.95

QUICK ORDER FORM

Fax order: 1-520-325-8743 and send this form.

Telephone orders: 1-877-731-6045 with credit card

Website Orders: Visit www.ChristineHarvey.com.

Mail To: Intrinsic Publishing, P.O. Box 26040, Tucson, AZ 85726 USA.

Please send the following books and tapes. I understand that I may return any of them for a full refund – no questions asked.

Books:

Qty: ___ Can A Girl Run for President? $14.95

Qty: ___ Secret's of the World's Top Sales Performers $6.95

Qty: ___ Your Pursuit of Profit $14.95

Qty: ___ Successful Selling $6.95

Qty: ___ Successful Motivation $14.95

Qty: ___ Public Speaking and Leadership Workbook $89.95

Tapes: (V = video) or (A = audio)

Qty: ___ Power Talk: V – $39.95 / A – $14.95

Qty: ___ Can A Girl Run For President?: V – $39.95 / A – $14.95

Qty: ___ 3 Steps to Business and Personal Success: A – $14.95

ക്ഷക്ഷക്ഷ

NAME: _____

ADDRESS: _____

CITY: _____ STATE: _____

ZIP/POST CODE: _____ COUNTRY: _____

E-MAIL ADDRESS: _____

TELEPHONE: _____ OR FAX _____

In case of shipping or order questions, we may need to contact you. Please list either email, telephone or fax; email preferred.

SALES TAX: Add 7% for books shipped to an Arizona address.

DISCOUNTS: *10% for 2 or more of the same title in books or tapes.*

SHIPPING BY AIR FOR US: $4 for first book/tape; $2 for each add'l.

FOR INTERNATIONAL: $9 for first book/tape; $5 for each add'l.

PAYMENT: ❑ Check or ❑ Card __VISA __M/C __AMEX

Card number: _____

Name on Card: _____ Exp. Date: __ / ____

BOOKS AND TAPES BY CHRISTINE HARVEY

Can A Girl Run For President?
Use the world as your arena as you develop your leadership. Step-by-step methods and advice for getting to the top by women around the world. Overcome limitations and reach your full potential. $14.95

Secret's of the World's Top Sales Performers
Ten people in 10 industries in 10 countries give you unique perspectives that can easily be adapted to your needs. A must for sales and non-sales people alike. 150,000 copies in 5 languages. $6.95

Your Pursuit of Profit: Christine Harvey with Bill Sykes
If you are in management, sales, run your own company, or simply want to advance, this book will help you. Pointers from hundreds of industries worldwide. 140,000 copies—8 languages. $14.95

Successful Selling
Looking for a new way to handle objections and closings? Would self-motivation and support systems really keep you going? Proven answers to these and other roadblocks. In 12 languages. $6.95

Successful Motivation
Do you want to motivate yourself and others to new levels? Seven methods for dealing with situations from difficult people to procrastination to raising productivity and job performance. $14.95

Public Speaking and Leadership Building
Pick this book up and use the methods today. Every situation for the beginner and the pro. Increase your ability step-by-step as your fears dissolve. In 5 languages. Workbook format. $89.95

Power Talk
Video or Audio
Powerful speaking and leadership techniques.
V – $39.95 / A – $14.95

Can A Girl Run For President?
Video or Audio
Christine Harvey's speech to American GS Leaders of Europe.
V – $39.95 / A – $14.95

3 Steps to Business and Personal Success – Audio
Interview with top sales performer Janet Lim, and a motivating speech about the Secrets of the World's Top Sales Performers. $14.95

QUICK ORDER FORM

Fax order: 1-520-325-8743 and send this form.

Telephone orders: 1-877-731-6045 with credit card

Website Orders: Visit www.ChristineHarvey.com.

Mail To: Intrinsic Publishing, P.O. Box 26040, Tucson, AZ 85726 USA.

Please send the following books and tapes. I understand that I may return any of them for a full refund – no questions asked.

Books:

Qty: ___ Can A Girl Run for President?　$14.95

Qty: ___ Secret's of the World's Top Sales Performers　$6.95

Qty: ___ Your Pursuit of Profit　$14.95

Qty: ___ Successful Selling　$6.95

Qty: ___ Successful Motivation　$14.95

Qty: ___ Public Speaking and Leadership Workbook $89.95

Tapes:　(V = video) or (A = audio)

Qty: ___ Power Talk: V – $39.95 / A – $14.95

Qty: ___ Can A Girl Run For President?: V – $39.95 / A – $14.95

Qty: ___ 3 Steps to Business and Personal Success: A – $14.95

෯෯෯෯෯෯

NAME: _____

ADDRESS: _____

CITY: _____ STATE: _____

ZIP/POST CODE: _____ COUNTRY: _____

E-MAIL ADDRESS: _____

TELEPHONE: _____ OR FAX _____

In case of shipping or order questions, we may need to contact you. Please list either email, telephone or fax; email preferred.

SALES TAX: Add 7% for books shipped to an Arizona address.

DISCOUNTS: *10% for 2 or more of the same title in books or tapes.*

SHIPPING BY AIR FOR US: $4 for first book/tape; $2 for each add'l.

FOR INTERNATIONAL: $9 for first book/tape; $5 for each add'l.

PAYMENT: ❑ Check or ❑ Card　__VISA　__M/C　__AMEX

Card number: _____

Name on Card: _____ Exp. Date: __ / ____

Books and Tapes by Christine Harvey

Can A Girl Run For President?
Use the world as your arena as you develop your leadership. Step-by-step methods and advice for getting to the top by women around the world. Overcome limitations and reach your full potential. $14.95

Secret's of the World's Top Sales Performers
Ten people in 10 industries in 10 countries give you unique perspectives that can easily be adapted to your needs. A must for sales and non-sales people alike. 150,000 copies in 5 languages. $6.95

Your Pursuit of Profit: Christine Harvey with Bill Sykes
If you are in management, sales, run your own company, or simply want to advance, this book will help you. Pointers from hundreds of industries worldwide. 140,000 copies—8 languages. $14.95

Successful Selling
Looking for a new way to handle objections and closings? Would self-motivation and support systems really keep you going? Proven answers to these and other roadblocks. In 12 languages. $6.95

Successful Motivation
Do you want to motivate yourself and others to new levels? Seven methods for dealing with situations from difficult people to procrastination to raising productivity and job performance. $14.95

Public Speaking and Leadership Building
Pick this book up and use the methods today. Every situation for the beginner and the pro. Increase your ability step-by-step as your fears dissolve. In 5 languages. Workbook format. $89.95

Power Talk
Video or Audio
Powerful speaking and leadership techniques.
V – $39.95 / A – $14.95

Can A Girl Run For President?
Video or Audio
Christine Harvey's speech to American GS Leaders of Europe.
V – $39.95 / A – $14.95

3 Steps to Business and Personal Success – Audio
Interview with top sales performer Janet Lim, and a motivating speech about the Secrets of the World's Top Sales Performers. $14.95

QUICK ORDER FORM

Fax order: 1-520-325-8743 and send this form.

Telephone orders: 1-877-731-6045 with credit card

Website Orders: Visit www.ChristineHarvey.com.

Mail To: Intrinsic Publishing, P.O. Box 26040, Tucson, AZ 85726 USA.

Please send the following books and tapes. I understand that I may return any of them for a full refund – no questions asked.

Books:

Qty: ___ Can A Girl Run for President? $14.95

Qty: ___ Secret's of the World's Top Sales Performers $6.95

Qty: ___ Your Pursuit of Profit $14.95

Qty: ___ Successful Selling $6.95

Qty: ___ Successful Motivation $14.95

Qty: ___ Public Speaking and Leadership Workbook $89.95

Tapes: (V = video) or (A = audio)

Qty: ___ Power Talk: V – $39.95 / A – $14.95

Qty: ___ Can A Girl Run For President?: V – $39.95 / A – $14.95

Qty: ___ 3 Steps to Business and Personal Success: A – $14.95

∽∽∽∽∽∽∽

NAME: _____

ADDRESS: _____

CITY: _____ STATE: _____

ZIP/POST CODE: _____ COUNTRY: _____

E-MAIL ADDRESS: _____

TELEPHONE: _____ OR FAX _____

In case of shipping or order questions, we may need to contact you. Please list either email, telephone or fax; email preferred.

SALES TAX: Add 7% for books shipped to an Arizona address.

DISCOUNTS: *10% for 2 or more of the same title in books or tapes.*

SHIPPING BY AIR FOR US: $4 for first book/tape; $2 for each add'l.

FOR INTERNATIONAL: $9 for first book/tape; $5 for each add'l.

PAYMENT: ❑ Check or ❑ Card __VISA __M/C __AMEX

Card number: _____

Name on Card: _____ Exp. Date: __ / ____